THE ROYAL HORTICULTURAL SOCIETY
PRACTICAL GUIDES

ANNUALS &
BIENNIALS

THE ROYAL HORTICULTURAL SOCIETY
PRACTICAL GUIDES

ANNUALS &
BIENNIALS

CHRISTOPHER GREY-WILSON

DORLING KINDERSLEY
LONDON • NEW YORK • SYDNEY • MOSCOW
www.dk.com

DK

LONDON, NEW YORK, MUNICH,
MELBOURNE, DELHI

PROJECT EDITOR Annelise Evans
ART EDITOR Ursula Dawson

SERIES EDITOR Gillian Roberts
SERIES ART EDITOR Stephen Josland

SENIOR MANAGING EDITOR Mary-Clare Jerram
MANAGING ART EDITOR Lee Griffiths

DTP DESIGNER Louise Paddick

PRODUCTION CONTROLLER Mandy Inness

First published in Great Britain in 2000
Reprinted 2003
by Dorling Kindersley Limited,
80 Strand, London WC2R 0RL

A Penguin Company

Copyright © 2000 Dorling Kindersley Limited, London

All rights reserved. No part of this publication may be reproduced, stored in a
retrieval system, or transmitted in any form or by any means, electronic, mechanical,
photocopying, recording, or otherwise, without the prior written permission
of the copyright owner.

A CIP catalogue record for this book is available from the British Library.
ISBN 0 7513 48643

Reproduced by Colourscan, Singapore
Printed and bound by Star Standard Industries, Singapore

Rosewarne
Learning Centre

See our complete catalogue at
www.dk.com

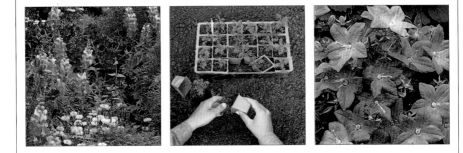

CONTENTS

Using Annuals and Biennials

What are Annuals and Biennials?

An annual plant, in botanical terms, is one that completes its life cycle, from the germinating seed to a mature flowering plant, followed by fruit-set and seed production, within a single growing season, often in a few short months. Annuals are therefore fast-growing plants and often produce a mass of colourful flowers. Biennials take two growing seasons to fulfil their life cycles, germinating in the first year and flowering, fruiting, and dying in the second.

Hardiness to Cold

Many annuals and biennials are fully hardy, so withstand freezing conditions, and can usually be sown directly in the garden, in autumn or early spring. Frost-hardy annuals and biennials tolerate some frost, to –5°C (23°F). They must be sown under glass in late winter or early spring, for planting out after the worst frosts, or in the open in mid-spring. Half-hardy annuals, including many bedding annuals such as petunias and nicotiana, will not stand frost; tender annuals dislike cold, below 5°C (41°F). These last two groups of annuals can be planted in the open garden only once all risk of frost has gone and soil temperatures have risen. They are ideal for warm sites, conservatories, or containers.

◄ HARDY ANNUAL
Many fast-growing, hardy annuals like this nasturtium, Tropaeolum *Alaska Series, produce a mass of colourful flowers within a few weeks from seed.*

◄ACCENTUATE THE VERTICAL *Mulleins and red orache bring instant height to a border.*

▲ BIENNIAL
*Typical biennials, including
the lovely common foxglove
(*Digitalis purpurea)*, form
a rosette of leaves in the first
year and send up flowering
stems in the second.*

▶ HALF-HARDY ANNUAL
A drift of Zinnia haageana
*'Persian Carpet' produces
a blaze of colour throughout
the summer months.*

Most annuals are easy to grow in the
garden, whether or not they have to be
started off under glass. They quickly form
a mass of colour, primarily in summer and
early autumn, although some flower in
spring. By sowing seed of each plant in
batches, the display can be extended over
many weeks. Annuals come in a huge range
of colours, sizes, and textures, so can be
used for many different styles of planting.

Gardeners value annuals for their bright
display of flowers, suited to modern small
gardens, for formal bedding schemes, and
for container planting, but some annuals

also make excellent cut flowers, foliage
plants, subjects for drying, or for enticing
insects and other wildlife into the garden.

The range of options can be extended
with biennials such as wallflowers and
some of the mulleins (*Verbascum*), whether
grown on over winter and then planted
out, or sown direct to flower the next year.

PERENNIALS GROWN AS ANNUALS
A number of short-lived garden perennials
(plants that flower for more than two
years) are grown from seed as annuals, to
flower in their first year. These include

TRADITIONAL FAVOURITES

ANNUALS	BIENNIALS	PERENNIALS GROWN AS ANNUALS
Centaurea cyanus	*Digitalis purpurea*	*Antirrhinum majus*
Clarkia amoena	*Eryngium giganteum*	*Begonia semperflorens*
Linum grandiflorum	*Erysimum cheiri*	*Impatiens walleriana*
Nigella damascena	*Verbascum chaixii*	

familiar plants such as the small bedding dahlias, busy Lizzies (*Impatiens*) including the New Guinea hybrids, and many types of pelargonium. Quite a few plants sold for annual bedding are in fact perennials. Although they can be discarded at the end of the season in cool or temperate climates, many can be overwintered under glass as plants, or as autumn-rooted cuttings.

GROWING PLANTS TOGETHER

Few gardens are devoted solely to annuals and biennials – these are just one element in a varied planting that may include trees, shrubs, perennials, and bulbs. Annuals are often grown on their own in a border for maximum impact, but can combine well with other plants – in containers, for instance, or to fill gaps in herbaceous beds.

Later in this book, you will find some suggested plantings for annuals and biennials in the garden. Alternatives can be found in Choice Annuals and Biennials (*see pp.60–77*), and good nurseries and garden centres should also offer an excellent selection of suitable plants and seed.

▲ TRADITIONAL
ANNUAL BORDER
This attractive border consists of vivid drifts of frost-hardy and half-hardy plants, such as coreopsis, dahlias, salpiglossis, and zinnias.

◄ A MIXED BORDER
An impression of a bank of wildflowers has been created here by mixing together some antirrhinums, cornflowers, and pansies with an informal planting of hardy perennials.

PLANTING IDEAS

THERE IS ROOM FOR ANNUALS AND BIENNIALS even in the smallest garden. Baskets, floral pillars, and windowboxes can be crammed with vibrant flowers and foliage to excite the eye for many months of the year. More plants can be infiltrated into the herbaceous border or scattered among shrubs to liven up permanent plantings with seasonal colour. A container brimful of petunias or pansies can be a stunning focal point in a courtyard, on a patio or balcony.

MIXING AND MATCHING PLANTS

If you have a large enough garden to devote an entire bed to a summer display, then an annual border can be the high point of the year. However, integrating annuals and biennials with other planting opens up a world of possible combinations of colour, form, and texture. For new beds, borders, or gardens, annuals and biennials, particularly bedding plants, are extremely useful for furnishing almost instant colour and interest while permanent members of the planting display establish.

The structure of existing borders is usually provided by small trees and shrubs, as well as herbaceous perennials. The look of the borders can be transformed from year to year by using annuals and biennials to ring the changes of the seasons. Most annuals are fairly shallow-rooted and thrive among deep-rooted perennials. Annuals grow best in an open, sunny situation and dislike being overshadowed by trees and shrubs so, in smaller gardens, some thinning of existing trees and shrubs may be needed to allow the annuals to perform at their best.

▲ PAINTING WITH PLANTS
The traditional way to grow annuals is to sow or plant them in drifts, to paint a seasonal bed or border with blocks of colour, as with this pretty Phlox drummondii *'Sternenzauber'.*

▶ ORNAMENTAL KITCHEN GARDEN
Annual English or pot marigolds and borage are perfect in an informal vegetable garden; as well as being colourful foils to these decorative cabbages, the flowers are edible.

However, a few annuals – especially busy Lizzies – prefer dappled shade and are ideal for brightening up more enclosed spots.

For instant height, use annuals and biennials with tall flower spikes, such as foxgloves, or even sunflowers. Annual climbers such as canary creepers or sweet peas can be encouraged to scramble over and through small shrubs, or up a wigwam of canes, to create a colourful focal point.

Felicitous plant associations can happen by chance if annuals and biennials are left to seed about the garden – simply weed out any plants that pop up in inappropriate

Tall annuals and biennials add temporary structure to a border

---

places – but it is worth planning to assure a successful display. Try mixing forget-me-nots, honesty, poached-egg plants, pansies, and wallflowers with spring-flowering bulbs, such as daffodils, hyacinths, and tulips, or, in summer, grow corn cockles, larkspurs, love-in-a-mist, and poppies with bulbs such as alliums, gladioli, and irises.

▲ DYNAMIC DUO
Brilliant yellow corn marigolds and hot red poppies, both quick-growing annuals, make a dramatic summer combination.

▼ GOOD ENOUGH TO EAT
Annual and perennial edible herbs (here nasturtiums, pansies, and English or pot marigolds, with perennial purple sage and variegated mint) are planted together in a bank of colour to form an appetizing alliance.

ANNUAL SEED MIXTURES

MOST ANNUALS ARE IDEAL for sowing directly in the garden, especially when a naturalistic effect is required, since the seeds of many different plants can be mixed and sown together. All you have to do is to prepare the soil, sow the seed mixture at the appropriate time, and then stand back and await the results. The consequent medley of pretty flowers of varying hues, forms, and heights will evoke the casual harmony of nature.

NATURAL BEAUTY

Many annuals, especially the species, have a simplicity of flower and form that lends itself to naturalistic schemes in the garden. Whereas blended seed mixtures produce displays that look a little out of place in a formal setting, they are perfect for borders in an informal or a cottage-garden style. Naturalistic mixes also attract insects and birds into the garden.

A patch of uncultivated or recently tilled soil in the garden, preferably one that has not been enriched with fertilizers, presents an opportunity to create a charming swathe of annuals that recalls wildflower meadows of times past. If the soil is tilled regularly, arable-land seed mixes will reappear for many years, so providing a recurring, but ever-changing, seasonal display.

Seed merchants supply an enormous range of attractive seed mixtures of annuals: for cool or hot colour schemes, for cutting, to grow for scent, wildflower mixtures, and quick-growing assortments for children to

> Change the look of your garden by sowing a new seed mixture each year

try. Yet half the fun is to make up your own mixture. For a successful blend, choose seeds of plants that will look good with one another and are about the same height, although some differences in height can result in a pleasingly tiered effect. Annuals with small flowers, such as daisies,

BLOWSY BORDER
This border, brimful of hardy annuals, relies on blues and purples, studded with a few bright colours, to create a softly pretty drift of flowers that will also attract pollinating insects.

◀ MEADOW MIX
*Annual species, such
as blue cornflowers,
white marguerites,
scarlet poppies,
and yellow corn
marigolds, create a
brilliantly coloured
summer meadow.*

▼ COTTAGE GARDEN
*Annuals are the
mainstay of old-style
cottage gardening, in
which beds spill over
with a colourful
patchwork of flower.*

or simple blooms such as poppies, will look
more natural than showy garden cultivars
like the double zinnias. Add seeds of
willowy annual grasses for an airy effect.
Above all, select types that mature at more
or less the same time, to gain and enjoy the
full impact of the blooms.

SOWING SEED MIXTURES

When preparing your own mixture, be sure
to mix the seeds thoroughly; adding fine
sand to the mix will help you to sow the
seeds thinly and evenly. Over-thick sowings
will require a good deal of thinning at the
seedling stage to ensure a good display. It
is also important to choose the right seed
mixture for your soil, otherwise the results
are likely to be disappointing. Specialist
wildflower firms sell annual mixtures, or
mixtures of annuals and perennials, for
many different soil types.

Half-hardy and tender annuals can be
sown direct in mild areas once the soil is
warm enough but, in cold and temperate
climates, plants need to be raised under
glass and planted out randomly to produce
the same effect as sowing a mixture.

PLANTS FOR COLOUR

THINK OF A COLOUR and you are almost bound to find an annual or biennial in that hue. Use the colour wheel (*right*) to help you explore the way in which colours relate to each other and the effects of different colour combinations in the garden. You can learn a lot about use of colour by visiting other gardens and noting the most pleasing colour associations.

COLOUR WHEEL

THE COLOUR WHEEL

Three primary colours – blue, yellow, and red – form the basis of the colour wheel. These blend together to produce secondary colours – purple, green, and orange – between them; where the segments meet are many gradations of shade and hue. Colours furthest apart on the wheel produce the strongest contrasts, such as purple and yellow or blue and orange. Using plants with hues from opposing segments of the colour wheel can produce a dazzling, and sometimes shocking, effect which may be lively and eye-catching from a distance. Some plants produce their own stark contrasts: the brilliant red flowers of the corn poppy contrast vividly with its own bright green foliage; some pansies strikingly combine hot yellows and deep purples in their blooms. In contrast, neighbouring

BASIC COLOURS
Plants of a single colour may be used in a monochrome planting, with toning shades of the same hue, or with other colours. Use white flowers as cooling highlights.

MOLUCCELLA LAEVIS

ZINNIA ELEGANS
'DREAMLAND SCARLET'

ERYSIMUM CHEIRI
'FIRE KING'

ESCHSCHOLZIA CALIFORNICA
'YELLOW CAP'

NEMESIA VERSICOLOR
'BLUE BIRD'

colours such as blue and green, or pink and purple, produce softer, more harmonious effects. For example, the pink flowers of a corn cockle find a subtle foil in its silky-haired, grey-green leaves, while the delicate blue flowers of love-in-a-mist are softened further by its finely dissected green foliage.

> ## If space is limited, sow a single species with mixed flower colours

When planning colour combinations, do not forget the importance of foliage: grey or silver foliage, such as that of *Senecio cineraria*, can subtly complement blue and white flowers; coleus (*Solenostemon*) has leaves in vivid golds, reds, and purples.

PLANNING COLOUR SCHEMES

Experimenting with colour when using annuals and biennials in the garden can be fun, but also daunting. It helps to work out the plant combinations roughly on paper before sowing or planting. Go for colour schemes that really appeal to you.

Your choice will also depend to some extent on the effect that you are trying to create. Interestingly, bold, hot colours such as orange and gold make plants much more prominent, whereas cool colours like pink, white, and blue have a more impressionistic effect and create an illusion of distance.

The impact of the planting will also be influenced by other features in the garden, especially the colours of surrounding trees and shrubs. The varying heights of the plants and their flowering periods will play a key role in the effectiveness of the design.

IPOMOEA PURPUREA 'GRANDPA OTT'

CLEOME HASSLERIANA 'HELEN CAMPBELL'

VIOLA 'ROMEO AND JULIET'
Some cultivars have flowers of harmonious mixed colours.

USING HOT COLOURS

H OT, VIBRANT COLOURS WORK wonderfully well in warmer countries, but vivid reds, yellows, and oranges, liberally used, can produce an impression of warmth, even during cool summers in more temperate zones. Among annuals and biennials, the hotter colours are almost exclusively restricted to summer- and autumn-flowering plants; they perfectly complement the autumnal foliage, with its reds, russets, and bronzes, of surrounding trees and shrubs.

SEASONAL BRILLIANCE

In early summer, the brilliant scarlet annual poppies display their tissue-paper blooms and the clear yellows and golds of the annual chrysanthemums are at their best. As the summer wears on, more and more brightly hued annuals appear, from the various sorts of marigold (*Calendula* and *Tagetes*) to the handsome rudbeckias in all colours from lemon-yellow to gold and rusty red, which prolong the season well

into autumn. From midsummer onwards, a succession of salvias in reds, purples and bright pinks, and similarly coloured penstemons, grace the garden. This vivid cornucopia of colour is brought to a close only by the first frosts of autumn.

Subtle is not the word to describe the exuberant reds, oranges, and yellows of summer annuals and biennials. You can use them to create hot spots in beds and borders that draw the eye along the garden.

GLOWING FOLIAGE
There is no need for dazzling flowers when the foliage is brightly hued, as with this bank of coleus, Solenostemon Wizard *Series. The leaves echo the yellow of the ivy,* Hedera helix *'Buttercup' behind. Each plant of coleus may display a slightly different combination of colours or patterns. Ideal for summer bedding in warmer gardens, coleus also make splendid container plants.*

▲ RED-HOT PINKS
Dianthus *Telstar Series comes
in a mixture of red and pink
shades; the lighter tones
accentuate the fiery scarlet,
providing a spectacular show.*

◄ EVERLASTING COLOUR
*The vividly clashing colours
of* Bracteantha bracteata *may
be preserved by drying them
to brighten winter days.*

Deep yellow and orange calendulas set among blood-red zinnias and tawny rudbeckias form a bold combination that certainly cannot be overlooked. The choice of warm-coloured annuals and biennials is almost endless, but it can be a mistake to overplay the hot colours. They may be simply too busy and hectic. Other, more subtle contrasts may often prove far more effective. For instance, bright orange and red shades can look splendid against the purple foliage of *Atriplex* or red-leaved *Celosia*, while deep purple salvias may be greatly enhanced by the yellow-green foliage of *Smyrnium*.

Contrasting flower form and shape may add interest, especially when upright spikes of plants such as golden verbascums are set against rounded flowerheads of plants such as pompon dahlias or African marigolds.

HOT-COLOURED ANNUALS

RED
Linum grandiflorum 'Rubrum'
Pelargonium Diamond Series
Salvia splendens

ORANGE
Mimulus Malibu Series
Rudbeckia hirta 'Marmalade'
Tithonia rotundifolia

YELLOW
Argemone mexicana
Helianthus annuus
Limnanthes douglasii

PURPLE
Digitalis purpurea
Nierembergia caerulea 'Purple Robe'
Petunia (many purple cultivars)

USING COOL COLOURS

MOST GARDENS NEED COOL BORDERS to give an airy feeling of freshness and space. However, a mass planting of annuals and biennials in cool colours, especially blue, white, and pale pink, may prove to be bland and uninspiring unless enhanced with pale and matt greens, subtle creams, and soft yellows. Occasionally, stronger, contrasting colours can be introduced as highlights or even deliberate clashes or disturbances in the overall harmony of the border.

PALE AND INTERESTING
Planting schemes in cool colours become very prominent and almost luminous in the dusk of evening and at night, when hot colours fade into the gloom. They also recede into the distance and create an impression of space in the garden.

When planning a cool combination, try not to mix too many blues and pale pinks: moderation in the choice of plants is the key to success, because too many different shades will look fussy rather than soothing.

COOL COMBINATIONS
Try blending the pure blue blooms and feathery green foliage of love-in-a-mist (*Nigella damascena*) with dainty corn cockles (*Agrostemma githago*), the delicate pastel shades of the tissue-thin petals of *Papaver rhoeas* 'Mother of Pearl', and the white mistiness of *Gypsophila elegans*. If more greens are required, think about adding some of the annual grasses, such as the fountain grass (*Pennisetum setaceum*). The whole effect of the planting can be light, restful, and meadow-like.

PURE WHITE BOUNDARIES
The white flowers of petunias and feverfew (Tanacetum parthenium) *against green foliage make a soft, yet elegant, edge to a pathway.*

COOL-COLOURED ANNUALS

CREAMS AND WHITES	*Felicia amelloides*	*Heliotropium arborescens*
Digitalis purpurea f. *albiflora*	*Nemophila menziesii*	
Dimorphotheca pluvialis	*Nigella damascena*	**PINKS**
Lavatera trimestris 'Mont Blanc'		*Cleome hassleriana* (pink forms)
	LILACS, MAUVES, AND VIOLETS	*Papaver rhoeas* 'Mother of Pearl'
Omphalodes linifolia	*Brachyscome iberidifolia*	
	Browallia speciosa	*Silene armeria*
BLUES	*Clarkia amoena*	*Silene coeli-rosa*
Ageratum houstonianum		

◄ STAR PLANT
Nemophila maculata *is a pretty little hardy annual that makes an excellent subject for the edge of a cool border. It is stunning with blue lobelias or Swan River daisies* (Brachyscome).

▼ A COOL BORDER
Lobelias, Nemesia *'Fragrant Cloud', and pansies create a study in blue and white, contrasted with the soft grey foliage of* Helichrysum petiolare *'Variegatum'.*

For a very dramatic display, try planting a border composed only of blue-flowered annuals and biennials. An all-white border can seem almost wintry, even at the height of summer. The occasional introduction of pleasing foliage plants, whether annual, biennial, or short-lived perennials, (for instance, silver-leaved *Senecio cineraria*

Deep green or purple foliage makes a dramatic contrast to pale blooms

or the fresh green of the burning bush (*Bassia scoparia* f. *trichophylla*) can heighten the sense of quiet beauty. The spiky biennial Miss Willmott's ghost (*Eryngium giganteum*) and the perennial lamb's ears (*Stachys byzantina*), with silver-grey, furry foliage, also offer contrasts in leaf colour and texture to highlight and complement the main colour scheme.

Above all, never be afraid to experiment. Annuals and biennials are only short-lived seasonal plants, so if you do not get it quite right one year, there is always the next.

ANNUALS AND BIENNIALS FOR DRYING

S PRING AND SUMMER ARE THE SEASONS in which annuals and biennials hold the
stage, but long after the summer flowers have withered away in the garden,
dried arrangements indoors can prolong the display and remind you of the
glories of the past summer. Many annuals and some biennials lend themselves
to drying. Carefully dried flowers retain their colour well and, if kept in a dry
atmosphere, will last for at least twelve months until the next harvest is ready.

PRESERVING PERFECTION

The vivid colours of fresh annual and
biennial flowers can become quite muted
in the drying process, but the subtle, earthy
tones of naturally dried flowers are very
pleasing. In contrast, commercially dried
flowers are often dyed in brash and
unnatural hues. The form and texture of
dried flowers is as important as the colours.
Look for strong shapes such as the elegant
cups of bells of Ireland (*Moluccella laevis*)
or the spiky bracts and leaves of sea holly
(*Eryngium*) and interesting textures, such

as the papery heads of strawflowers
(*Bracteantha bracteata*). Seedheads can
look as handsome as flowers when dried,
whether displayed in arrangements on their
own or mixed with dried flowers.

To avoid spoiling displays in the flower
garden, try setting aside a small plot (part
of the vegetable garden, for instance) to
grow annuals and biennials specifically for
drying. Here, they can be sown and grown
in serried ranks until they are ready to be
cut; sow grasses more thickly than usual so
that their slender stems support each other.

LONG-LASTING COLOUR
Statice (Limonium sinuatum)
is a long-flowering annual,
widely used as a dried flower
and available in a variety
of colours. Cut sprays can be
hung upside-down in bunches
to dry and have a decorative
charm all their own.

POPPY PEPPER POTS
*The fat seed capsules
of the opium poppy
(Papaver somniferum)
are among the most
decorative of all
annuals. Dried pods
look very dramatic
sprayed gold or silver
and used in winter
wreaths and garlands.*

DRYING FLOWERS AND FRUITS

Take care to select flowers for drying that are half-open; most fully mature flowers will not dry well. Plants with large, delicate flowers, such as clarkias or poppies, are not suitable for drying. Cut single flowers or sprays with long stems, and strip off large leaves and damaged or overblown flowers.

Tie the stems in small bunches with soft string or raffia and hang them upside-down to dry in an airy, warm, dry place, out of direct sun. Once thoroughly dried, cut the bunches down and make them up into

Use dried flowers and fruits in swags, wreaths, posies, and pot-pourris

arrangements. Take care when handling dried flowers because they are quite fragile.

The method for drying and preserving fruits is the same as for flowers. The best time to collect fruits and seed capsules for drying is when they are fully mature and are just starting to dry out naturally. If left too long in the garden, they will often become discoloured or marked.

Annual grasses are also excellent for drying. The timing is critical: cut too early and the stems will be too soft and thin to support the heads, but cut too late and the spikelets will begin to fall apart at the slightest touch. Generally, the best time to cut grasses for drying is when the lower spikelets in the heads come into flower (generally signified by the appearance of the yellow or cream stamens).

GOOD PLANTS FOR DRYING

Bracteantha bracteata	*Onopordum acanthium*
Consolida ajacis	*Psylliostachys suworowii*
Eryngium giganteum	
Gomphrena globosa	*Trachelium caeruleum*
Limonium sinuatum	*Xeranthemum annuum*
Moluccella laevis	

LUNARIA ANNUA

PROLONGING THE SEASON

A**FTER THE RICH DISPLAYS OF BLOOM** have faded, many flowering annuals also produce very decorative seedheads, changing the focus of the display from lush colour to starker forms, textures, and subtle, harvest tones well into the autumn and winter. Annual grasses echo the mood, their plumes becoming more feathery and bleached as they go to seed. A few annuals and biennials add spots of colour with glossy fruits in festive scarlet.

FRUITFUL HARVEST

Some annuals, such as French marigolds (*Tagetes*), busy Lizzies (*Impatiens*), and petunias, are grown only for their flowers, so deadheading is important in prolonging the display. However, if you avoid the temptation to clear away other annuals at the end of summer, you can enjoy annuals with ornamental fruits and the fascinating variety of those with attractive seedheads.

Bring zest to the summer border with the chilli pepper (*Capsicum annuum*) – its many cultivars have tapering fruits in fiery reds, purples, and yellows. You could continue the theme indoors with the bright winter cherry (*Solanum pseudocapsicum*).

The scope for using seedheads is even greater. Annual honesty (*Lunaria annua*) has tissue-thin, papery discs with a silvery sheen; those of love-in-a-mist (*Nigella damascena*) look like little balloons, while those of poppies (*Papaver*) resemble pepper pots. Californian poppies (*Eschscholzia*) have long, slender pods that curve into a sickle shape when ripe. Other annuals, like *Onopordum acanthium*, have long-lasting,

▲ VERSATILE SUNFLOWER
This gaudy annual daisy (here Helianthus *'Pastiche') is a star performer in the garden, is excellent for cutting or for drying as a winter decoration, and has edible seeds.*

▶ DECORATIVE HERB
Dill is an aromatic annual widely used as a culinary herb. The flat clusters of seeds are very ornamental and can be dried for winter use.

▲ QUAKING GRASS
This fast-growing annual grass is named after its locket-shaped seedheads which rattle in the slightest breeze.

◄ AGEING GRACEFULLY
Grasses such as foxtail barley fluff out and fade to beige as they go to seed, and add lightness to plants like these perennials, Gaura lindheimeri.

thistle-like seedheads. The biggest and boldest of them all is the sunflower, with flat discs of hundreds of symmetrically arranged seeds, a study in geometry.

Besides their ornamental value, the fruits and seedheads are the source of seed, that may be collected for the following year's display (*see pp.56–57*) or in some cases for culinary use, or left on the plant over the winter to provide food for wild birds.

GRACIOUS GRASSES

The sleek, silky, or distinctly fuzzy flower clusters or spikelets of annual grasses improve with age, becoming fluffier and more delicately coloured as they go to seed. They often persist for months into winter. Grasses tone down excesses of hot summer borders and can create a marvellously impressionistic look when used with pastel flowers. Later, rimed with frost, they take on an ethereal magic all their own.

RECOMMENDED

DECORATIVE FRUITS
Capsicum annuum; Solanum pseudocapsicum

DECORATIVE SEEDPODS
Argemone; Atriplex hortensis
Cardiospermum halicacabum
Consolida ajacis; Dipsacus fullonum
Eccremocarpus scaber;
Glaucium corniculatum; Lablab purpureus
Papaver somniferum; Ricinus communis
Scabiosa

EDIBLE SEEDS
Anethum graveolens; Coriandrum sativum
Foeniculum vulgare; Helianthus annuus
Zea mays

GRASSES
Briza maxima; Hordeum jubatum
Lagurus ovatus; Pennisetum setaceum
Setaria italica

ANNUAL CLIMBING PLANTS

SOME OF THE MOST BEAUTIFUL AND POPULAR of the flowering annuals are climbers. Most are fast-growing and excellent for punctuating a border with a pillar of bloom, dressing an arch or pergola, disguising an unsightly structure, or creating an exuberant wall of summer colour. Combined with bushy annuals, they extend the surge of flower upwards, and if allowed to scramble among herbaceous perennials and shrubs, they add a pleasing touch of informality.

CROWNING GLORIES

The queen of annual climbing plants is undoubtedly the sweet pea (*Lathyrus odoratus*), prized for its beautiful, sweetly perfumed flowers in many attractive hues. Although it dislikes hot, dry areas, it grows to perfection in many gardens. Few annual climbers make finer cut flowers. Where sweet peas fail, other annual climbers will thrive, producing a mass of lovely blooms and fresh green foliage in a short space of time to add to the sense of abundance in the spring and summer garden. Morning

SWEET PEAS

Sweet peas are often trained up a 2.5m (8ft) wigwam of canes or on netting suspended from a row of canes.

Wigwam made of 8–10 canes inserted in a circle and tied together at top

---

Liven up the evergreen of ivy with bright blooms of annual climbers

---

glories (*Ipomoea*) are especially impressive, being rampant growers that open vividly coloured trumpets over a long season.

Most annual climbers can also be grown in large containers to form a feature for courtyards or patios, or allowed to creep

PRACTICAL TIPS

• Most annual climbers dislike being transplanted, so sow several seeds to a small pot, thin out to one seedling, and grow on.
• Alternatively, if it is warm enough, direct sow seed in the garden where the climbers are to flower (this applies to all annual climbers except *Cardiospermum*, *Cobaea*, *Rhodochiton*, and *Thunbergia*).
• Place supports in position in the garden before direct sowing or planting, to avoid damaging young plants, especially the roots.
• Allow plenty of space and headroom – annual climbers can be very vigorous.
• Pinch out growing tips of young plants to encourage bushy growth.
• Deadhead the plants regularly to prolong the flower display, unless they are being grown for their fruits or seedpods.

▲ DRAMA QUEEN
Rhodochiton atrosanguineus, although perennial, is grown as an annual for the dramatic hue of its flowers, with their long, purple-black corollas.

Rosewarne
Learning Centre

◄ ELEGANT ARCH
Spanish flag (Ipomoea lobata) drapes an arch in exotic red blooms that mature through summer to orange and gold.

through beds among perennials or shrubs. In cooler climates, they are superb for decorating conservatories, where they add dappled shade as well as jazzy colour.

SUPPORTING ANNUAL CLIMBERS

Most annual climbers reach 2–3m (6–10ft) or so and all are self-supporting. Some, such as morning glories and black-eyed Susan (*Thunbergia alata*) have twining stems; sweet peas and eccremocarpus cling with delicate tendrils, while climbing tropaeolums and rhodochiton fasten their leaf-stalks around any slender support.

The climbers can be trained up formal supports such as obelisks or pergolas, along wooden trellis, chain-link fencing, or wires fixed to a wall, or through a simple cane wigwam or cylinder of wire netting. Tie in young plants with wire rings or twine until they take hold. For an informal look, push large, branched stems (pea sticks) into the ground to form an attractive thicket.

▲ CHEAP AND CHEERFUL
As well as providing thick cover in weeks, Canary creeper (Tropaeolum peregrinum) has a mass of small, but pretty, fringed flowers.

SCENTED ANNUALS AND BIENNIALS

FRAGRANCE IS ALL TOO OFTEN OVERLOOKED in the rush to find spectacular combinations of colour. But, from light hints of perfume drifting from a border to headier fragrances pervading the air, scent is the essence of the spring and summer garden. When it comes to scent, annuals and biennials have it in plenty. Fragrant plants also entice beneficial insects such as butterflies and bees into the garden, to pollinate the flowers and contribute to the soothing scene.

FLOWERS AND FOLIAGE

Any annual seed mixtures used in the garden or annual border should include scented plants. A freshly picked posy would not be complete without at least a few fragrant blooms. When choosing annuals and biennials for scent, bear in mind that not all forms of a plant are necessarily fragrant: for instance, the white forms of the tobacco plant (*Nicotiana*) are strongly perfumed, while most other cultivars have little or no scent. Petunias are the same, with the blue and purple flowers more generously scented that other colours.

In some annuals, such as tobacco plants and stocks (*Matthiola*), the scent is mainly produced during the evening and at night, making the garden a balmy retreat in which to stroll just before sunset. They are also good placed near windows, so that their perfume can drift into the house at night.

A few annuals and biennials are not noted for their flowers, but are still prized because of the power of their perfume; mignonette (*Reseda odorata*) is one such plant, and is intoxicatingly sweet.

Of course, not all plants in the annual garden have scented flowers. Some have leaves that are aromatic, especially when they are bruised. These are best grown in containers or near paths, so that they are regularly brushed against – try scented-leaved pelargoniums, or for a more pungent scent, French marigolds (*Tagetes*).

▲ EVENING PERFUME
Cultivars of Matthiola incana *are grown as annuals and release a strong scent at dusk.*

► SWEET AND LOW
Grow sweet alyssum, here Lobularia maritima *Easter Bonnet Series, near a path to enjoy its sweet scent.*

ATTRACTING WILDLIFE

Scented annuals and biennials are some of the best plants for attracting wildlife, especially insects and birds, into a garden. The two most important attributes a flower needs to entice insects are scent and colour. The sheer volume of fragrant, colourful flowers borne by annuals and biennials, especially old "cottage-garden" species such as honesty (*Lunaria annua*) and

> Day-flying moths visit petunias; night-flying moths like tobacco plants

phlox, makes them beacons for insects. Bees are attracted particularly to blue and yellow, while moths go for white.

As well as scent, flowers that produce plenty of pollen, especially large daisies, are particularly appealing to beetles and beneficial flies, including hoverflies. Having more insects in the garden draws in other wildlife such as birds and small mammals, to make the garden a true haven for all.

▲ BEE HONEYPOT
Two-lipped flowers, such as those of the annual clary (Salvia viridis) *are good for bringing the soothing buzz of bees into the summer garden.*

◄ SPRING INVITATION
The poached-egg plant (Limnanthes douglasii) *attracts early butterflies and bees into the spring garden with its rich store of sweet nectar.*

PLANTING PLANS AND STYLES

CHOOSING A STYLE OF PLANTING

ANNUALS AND BIENNIALS ARE EXCELLENT for producing quick colour in the garden in a range of styles. They can be impressive on their own or can be infiltrated among more permanent plants, but are best when used in harmony with the surrounding planting style. Most need a sunny position, or one in part-shade, and are usually unfussy about soil type, provided it is well-drained. The following pages demonstrate planting ideas for beds, borders, and containers.

ANNUALS AND BIENNIALS IN BORDERS

The traditional way to use annuals and biennials is to devote an entire border or bed to them and create a dazzling display of form and colour in the spring and summer months. They remain an essential element of cottage gardening, where plants of various shapes, heights, and colours intermingle in informal borders with complete abandon. If you do not have room for a border that will be bare for part of the year, try adding a blaze of seasonal texture and colour by using annuals and biennials as space-fillers in herbaceous borders and shrubberies. They can also be used to charming effect in new gardens, while more permanent plantings establish.

◄ BLUE MOOD *Warm colours used in a limited palette and varying forms can look bold without being busy. Here, the golden mop-heads of coreopsis and African marigolds meander through drifts of tall blue and white salvia spikes and dainty mauve verbenas.*

◄ SUMMER BORDER *Annuals bring a medley of hot colours to liven up the permanent planting.*

THE ANNUAL BORDER

This summer border is devoted to hardy annuals, direct sown in a sunny, sheltered site. The plants are stepped from the yew hedge down to the front, where blue anchusas and convolvulus vie with vibrant eschscholzias. Behind them, white rain daisies compete with delicate poppies and nigellas and papery bracteantha heads for grace. At the back, tall consolida spikes and refined pink agrostemma contrast with white lavatera and brazen rudbeckia.

PLANTING PLAN

1 *Agrostemma githago* 'Milas', 70–80cm (28–32in) tall
2 *Rudbeckia hirta*, 70–90cm (28–36in) tall
3 *Lavatera trimestris* 'Mont Blanc', 60–80cm (24–32in)
4 *Consolida ajacis* Imperial Series 90–120cm (36–48in)
5 *Dimorphotheca pluvialis*, 20–30cm (8–12in) tall
6 *Bracteantha bracteata*, 80–90cm (32–36in) tall
7 *Papaver rhoeas* Shirley Series, 60–70cm (24–28in) tall
8 *Nigella damascena* Persian Jewels Series, 45cm (18in)
9 *Anchusa capensis* 'Blue Angel', 20cm (8in) tall
10 *Eschscholzia californica*, 30cm (12in) tall
11 *Convolvulus tricolor* 'Royal Ensign', 20–30cm (8–12in)

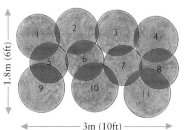

1.8m (6ft)

3m (10ft)

Rudbeckia hirta has stiff, leafy stems and bold yellow daisies with conical purple-brown centres, making it a good plant for cutting.

Agrostemma githago 'Milas', a corn cockle, bears deep plum-pink flowers on slender, silky-grey stems in early and midsummer.

Dimorphotheca pluvialis, or rain daisy, is easy to grow and has glistening white flowers, flushed violet beneath.

Anchusa capensis 'Blue Angel', or Cape alkanet, with its enchanting mass of small, brilliant blue flowers, is an excellent bee plant.

Bracteantha bracteata, or straw-flower, has papery everlasting flowers that persist well into autumn and are ideal for drying.

MORE CHOICES

TALL (over 90cm/36in)
Atriplex hortensis
Malope trifida
Tropaeolum majus

MEDIUM
(30–90cm/12–36in)
Antirrhinum majus
Borago officinalis
Chrysanthemum carinatum

Echium vulgare
Gypsophila elegans
Reseda odorata

SMALL (below 30cm/12in)
Calendula officinalis
Iberis umbellata
Layia platyglossa
Linum grandiflorum

ESCHSCHOLZIA
CALIFORNICA
California poppies begin to dazzle in early summer; regular deadheading prolongs the show well into autumn.

Lavatera trimestris 'Mont Blanc' forms a compact bush, unfurling a succession of virginal white, mallow blooms from summer to autumn.

Consolida ajacis, the larkspur, sends up stiff stems of crammed flower spikes in hues of blue, white, pink, purple, and red; all are good for cutting and drying.

Nigella damascena Persian Jewels Series, or love-in-a-mist, is a cottage garden favourite, with its feathery foliage, white, blue, and pink flowers, and pretty seed pods.

CONVOLVULUS TRICOLOR
'Royal Ensign' is a non-climbing, bushy bindweed. Each flower opens in sun and lasts one day, but many more appear all summer through.

Papaver rhoeas Shirley Series is a delightful selection of corn poppies, mostly in pastel shades of pink, rose, orange, and mauve.

A MIXED BORDER

In this informal herbaceous border, annuals and biennials intermingle easily with perennials. Tall spikes of verbascums and biennial foxgloves soar through bold clumps of perennial campanulas and leucanthemum daisies.

Below, clouds of annual eschscholzias, centaureas, linums, and lobelias drift between perennial achilleas, bergenias, salvias, and sedums to lift the border with seasonal colour. A pyramid of blue ipomoea adds a final flourish.

LINUM GRANDIFLORUM '*Rubrum*', *an annual flax, has delicate wand-like stems and eye-catching flowers that last all summer through.*

Digitalis purpurea, the wild foxglove, has tall spikes of purple, bee-beloved flowers. Look out for the self-sown seedlings in future years.

Sedum spectabile, or iceplant, forms a succulent mound of grey-green foliage, evergreen in milder areas. Its pink or purple flowers appear in late summer and are irresistible to butterflies.

Achillea filipendulina 'Gold Plate', a yarrow, bears its flattened flowerheads on stiff stems; they are long-lasting and excellent for drying.

Salvia × superba is a perennial sage. It forms clumps of upright stems bearing spikes of long-lasting, deep blue flowers.

Lobelia 'Crystal Palace' is a low and bushy annual. It is popular for edging a border because it flowers from early summer into autumn.

Eschscholzia lobbii is a dainty California poppy, making low mounds of delicate, ferny foliage adorned with masses of small, satin-yellow poppies.

Centaurea cyanus, the annual cornflower, is valued for its frilled flowers in shades of pink, purple, blue, and white; use a more dwarf form for the front of the border.

PLANTING PLAN

1 *Verbascum chaixii*, 100–130cm (39–52in) tall
2 *Achillea filipendulina* 'Gold Plate', 100cm (39in)
3 *Digitalis purpurea*, 100–140cm (39–54in) tall
4 *Ipomoea tricolor* 'Heavenly Blue', 2–3m (6–10ft)
5 *Lavatera trimestris*, 70–90cm (28–36in) tall
6 *Salvia* x *superba*, 80–90cm (32–36in) tall
7 *Sedum spectabile*, 40–50cm (16–20in) tall
8 *Campanula persicifolia*, 80–90cm tall
9 *Centaurea cyanus*, 60–90cm (2–3ft) tall
10 *Leucanthemum* x *superbum*, 90–100cm (36–39in)
11 *Lobelia* 'Crystal Palace', 10–20cm (4–8in) tall
12 *Eschscholtzia lobbii*, 15cm (6in) tall
13 *Linum grandiflorum* 'Rubrum', 45cm (18in) tall
14 *Bergenia* 'Silberlicht', 30–40cm (12–16in) tall

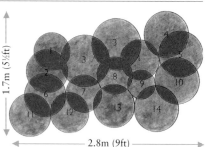

1.7m (5½ft)

2.8m (9ft)

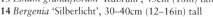

Campanula persicifolia has white or blue bells from early to late summer if deadheaded.

Verbascum x **chaixii**, a perennial mullein grown as a biennial, has spires of saucer-shaped, clear yellow flowers rising from coarse, grey basal rosettes of leaves.

IPOMOEA TRICOLOR 'Heavenly Blue', a morning glory, climbs to 3m (10ft) in one summer, and requires a minimum of 5°C (41°F).

Lavatera trimestris, an annual in the mallow family, unfurls a succession of silky, pink or white, funnel-shaped blooms all summer long.

MORE CHOICES

TALL (over 90cm/36in)
Silybum marianum
Tithonia rotundifolia

MEDIUM
(30–90cm/12–36in)
Scabiosa atropurpurea
Tanacetum parthenium

SMALL (below 30cm/12in)
Linaria maroccana
Phacelia campanularia

Leucanthemum x **superbum**, a bold, clump-forming perennial, produces large, yellow-centred daisies that are excellent for cutting.

Bergenia 'Silberlicht' has pink sprays of flowers in the spring, but its chief value lies in its bold, leathery, evergreen leaves.

FORMAL BEDDING

T HE DISCIPLINE OF FORMAL BEDDING forms a stark contrast to the informality of the annual or mixed border. Traditionally, large beds are filled with clearly delineated blocks of massed annuals and short-lived perennials, in simple geometric designs or more complex patterns and knots, to create a fresh scheme each year. The planting plan overleaf follows the same principles of clean lines and blocks of single colours, but on a scale suitable for a smaller garden.

CREATING A FORMAL STYLE

Formal designs are best in an open, sunny, but not exposed, position where they can be appreciated from all sides. The soil also needs to be well-drained, yet moisture-retentive. Many more modern annuals lend themselves to formal bedding because they are uniform in shape and vibrant of colour. More dwarf, compact cultivars are ideal, as well as those with a long flowering season. Large, bold flowers or foliage can be partnered with smaller types in similar or contrasting colours. Some entrancing effects can also be created using blends of muted colour. Finally, bear in mind that formal bedding is most effective if all the plants reach their peak at the same time.

MAKING A FORMAL BED

• Draw the design to scale on graph paper – avoid making it too complicated or fussy.
• Mark out the chosen pattern on the ground using canes and string, or sand.
• Choose plants for any permanent boundary with care; they must remain reasonably small and not mind regular clipping.
• Transplant annuals, especially half-hardy ones, into the bed rather than direct sow.
• Remember to use foliage plants as well as those with good flower forms or colours.
• Trim and deadhead plants regularly to keep the design looking neat and clearly defined.
• Ensure that the bed never dries out, which will tend to make the growth uneven.

◀FOCUS ON FORM
Rounded banks of Leucanthemum *'Show Star' edge a formal bed dominated by the flamboyant blooms and foliage of canna lilies. Spikes of annual salvia hug their flanks and the red of the cannas is echoed by mixed pelargoniums in neighbouring beds.*

◀CARPET BEDDING *A swirling pattern of silver* Senecio cineraria *and red* Begonia semperflorens.

A FORMAL BED

Here a square design is enclosed by dwarf box, neatly clipped for a strong line, and surrounded by gravel. The centrepiece is a ricinus with large, bronze leaves that effectively sets off the drooping tassels of amaranthus.

Around them, opposing triangles of violet salvias and pink pelargoniums jostle for attention. Low edging strips of golden tagetes and salmon-pink impatiens end in corner blocks of cool blue lobelias and ageratums.

PLANTING PLAN

1 *Buxus sempervirens* 'Suffruticosa', 1m (3ft) tall
2 *Ageratum houstonianum* 'Adriatic', 15–20cm (6–8in) tall
3 *Impatiens walleriana* Super Elfin Series, 15–20cm (6–8in)
4 *Lobelia* 'Cambridge Blue', 15cm (6in) tall
5 *Pelargonium* 'Multibloom Pink', 30–40cm (12–16in) tall
6 *Tagetes* 'Golden Gem', 20cm (8in) tall
7 *Amaranthus caudatus*, 60–90cm (2–3ft) tall
8 *Ricinus communis*, 100–120cm (39–48in) tall
9 *Salvia splendens* Cleopatra Series, 30cm (12in) tall

3m (10ft)

3m (10ft)

AMARANTHUS CAUDATUS
This dramatic plant has coarse leaves and splendid, pendent tassels of blood-red flowers, hence its common name, love-lies-bleeding.

Salvia splendens Cleopatra Series is a violet-flowered sage. It makes a neat, bushy plant and flowers all through the summer.

RECOMMENDED HEDGING PLANTS

The best hedging plants for use in formal bedding schemes are dwarf forms that are able to withstand regular clipping. Evergreens are most often used, to provide a permanent framework in which to plant new bedding each year. The hedge may take three or four years after planting to reach the desired height and shape.

Buxus sempervirens
'Suffruticosa'
Lavandula angustifolia
(compact forms)

Lonicera nitida
Santolina chamaecyparissus
Satureja montana
Teucrium fruticans
Thymus × citriodorus
Thymus vulgaris

Ricinus communis, the castor oil plant, is a branching shrub often grown as an annual feature plant. It has impressive foliage, which is large-lobed, bronzed-red, purple, or deep green.

Lobelia 'Cambridge Blue' is a popular plant for bedding, especially edging, because it forms compact clumps with a profusion of pale blue flowers.

Buxus sempervirens 'Suffruticosa', like all box, is a slow-growing evergreen, ideal for hedging. It can reach 1m (3ft), but can be kept to half that height by clipping it twice a year.

Tagetes 'Golden Gem' is a Signet marigold, producing flowers that last for many days.

Pelargonium 'Multibloom Pink', although a tender perennial, is widely grown as an annual, flowering quickly and lavishly from seed.

AGERATUM HOUSTONIANUM 'Adriatic', and other dwarf forms of the floss flower, make tidy little domes of foliage that are smothered in powder-puff flowers for many weeks.

Impatiens walleriana, or busy Lizzie, has fine dwarf forms, including this one with showy, salmon-pink blooms. It flowers more freely if regularly deadheaded.

Planting in Containers

MANY ANNUALS, BIENNIALS, AND PERENNIALS grown as annuals thrive in containers. They are ideal for small gardens, creating focal points in courtyards and on patios, filling gaps in summer borders, and adorning walls and windowsills. As the plants in one container fade, another can replace it, keeping a display at the height of perfection for many months. A variety of ideas for pretty plantings in containers are shown on the following pages.

Choosing Appropriate Containers

The choice of container is very much a personal one. A huge variety is now available in simple or ornate styles and in all colours of the rainbow, including those made of concrete, pottery, terracotta, plastic, metal, and wood. As well as pots and tubs, make use of wall space by filling hanging and wall baskets. Another option is a flower pillar or column that can be planted up with dozens of plants to create a spectacular display of bloom in a small space. For those without a garden, a windowbox, properly secured, can sustain a surprisingly large variety of plants.

When choosing containers, consider how they complement the colours and textures of the plants and the environment in which they will be placed. If grouping containers, do not use too many different styles and colours, otherwise the effect will be fussy.

PRACTICAL TIPS
• Choose containers that are large and deep enough to allow the plants' roots to develop.
• Smaller containers dry out more rapidly and require more frequent watering.
• Place larger containers in position before filling them – they can become very heavy.
• Choose a moisture-retentive compost, such as a soil-based potting compost.
• Add moisture-retentive granules and slow-release fertilizers to keep all the plants in vigorous growth for as long as possible.
• Locate containers in a sheltered position in sun or part shade (busy Lizzies, *Impatiens*, flower best in dappled shade).
• Keep drainage holes free from blockage by raising the container off the ground by 15cm (6in); half-bricks are ideal for this.
• Ensure that baskets, pillars, and other wall-mounted containers are securely anchored.

◀ SIMPLE CHARM
The more delicate delights among the annuals, such as these pansies, Viola *'Sorbet Yellow Frost', are perhaps best enjoyed planted individually in pots, unhindered by gaudier plants.*

◀ CASCADE OF BLOOM *Baskets and pots brim over with lobelia, busy Lizzies, and pelargoniums.*

A GROUP OF CONTAINERS

With regular feeds and deadheading, this display, in pots ranging in size from 23–75cm (9–30in), will last until autumn. The focal point of the group is formed by thunbergias clambering up a cane tripod. More height and volume comes from slender nicotianas and lush pelargoniums. Spreading and trailing lobelias, suteras, tropaeolums, and verbenas create more variations of form and colour while softening the hard edges of the containers.

Thunbergia alata is a free-flowering, twining climber. Its flowers may be apricot, pink, white, cream, or orange, but always have black eyes, hence its name, black-eyed Susan.

Lobelia 'Sapphire has slender, trailing stems and ample, two-lipped flowers of deep sapphire-blue.

Scaevola aemula 'New Wonder' is like lobelia, but more spreading than trailing, with larger and coarser blue flowers.

NICOTIANA 'LIME GREEN'
This tobacco plant has flowers of an unusual yellow-green, which is a superb foil for purples and reds. They also release a wonderful fragrance at night.

Tropaeolum majus 'Hermine Grashoff' has tumbling foliage and scented, showy, double orange-red flowers. Unusually, it cannot be raised from seed; take stem-tip cuttings from it instead.

Sutera grandiflora 'Sea Mist' has delicate, spreading and trailing stems and a profusion of tiny flowers, perfect for tumbling over the edge of a container.

PLANTING PLAN

1 *Nicotiana* 'Lime Green', 50–60cm (20–24in)
2 *Tropaeolum majus* 'Hermine Grashoff',
   20–30cm (8–12in) tall
3 *Sutera grandiflora* 'Sea Mist', 15–30cm
   (6–12in) tall
4 *Thunbergia alata*, 2–3m (6–10ft) tall
5 *Lobelia* 'Sapphire', 20cm (8in) tall
6 *Scaevola aemula* 'New Wonder', 20–30cm
   (8–12in) tall
7 *Gazania* Daybreak Series, 20cm (8in) tall
8 *Impatiens* Super Elfin Series, 20–50cm (8–20in) tall
9 *Pelargonium* 'Multibloom Pink', 40–60cm (16–24in) tall
10 *Mimulus* Malibu Series, 20–50cm (8–20in) tall
11 *Verbena* 'Imagination', 20–30cm (8–12in) tall
12 *Torenia fournieri* 'Blue Moon', 20–40cm (8–16in) tall

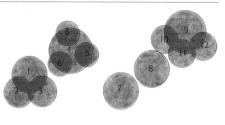

MORE CHOICES

BUSHY
Browallia speciosa
Salpiglossis sinuata
Schizanthus pinnatus

TRAILING
Bidens ferulifolia
Sanvitalia procumbens

FOLIAGE
Helichrysum petiolare
Solenostemon scutellarioides

Mimulus Malibu Series, or monkey flower, thrives in moist compost. Its cream, yellow, orange, pink, or red trumpets are often nicely spotted.

Pelargonium 'Multibloom Pink' is one of a number of modern bushy, very free-flowering pot geraniums, perfect for all containers.

Gazania Daybreak Series is a striking, tufted plant with daisies in pink, white, orange, yellow, or bronze, that open in sun.

Torenia 'Blue Moon' is a bushy annual with two-toned blue and purple flowers that persist into autumn.

Verbena 'Imagination' has a semi-trailing habit, producing bright clusters of blooms in deep violet-blue.

Impatiens Super Elfin Series, a form of the popular busy Lizzie, is perfect for filling a container by itself, with its hues of red, pink, orange, mauve, or white.

WINDOWBOX AND HANGING BASKET

Like all containers, these require daily watering and regular deadheading and feeding to keep the plants at their best. Special fastenings are now available for lowering hanging baskets to make access easier. Never be afraid to pack a container full of annuals, especially hanging baskets; they rarely look good when underplanted. Hanging baskets look lush brimming with a single, vigorous subject, but windowboxes are more effective with a mix of plants.

PLANTING PLAN FOR WINDOWBOX

1 *Sutera grandiflora* 'Knysna Hills', 30cm (12in)
2 *Exacum affine*, 20–30cm (8–12in) tall
3 *Torenia fournieri* 'Blue Moon', 40cm (16in)
4 *Tagetes* 'Tangerine Gem', 20cm (8in) tall
5 *Lobelia* 'Snowball', 20cm (8in) tall
6 *Brachyscome iberidifolia*, 40cm (16in) tall
7 *Verbena* 'Tapien Pink', 20cm (8in) tall
8 *Begonia semperflorens* hybrids, 30cm (12in)
9 *Impatiens walleriana* Tempo Series, 23cm (9in) tall

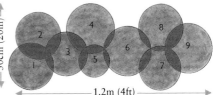

50cm (20in)

1.2m (4ft)

Tagetes 'Tangerine Gem', a Signet marigold, is a sturdy, pungent-leaved annual with long-lasting daisies of bright tangerine-orange.

Lobelia 'Snowball' is a bushy lobelia with pale green foliage and a mass of dashing white flowers.

Exacum affine, or Persian violet, is most often grown as a house plant, but looks just as good in a summer windowbox. It has bright green, fleshy foliage and purple-blue flowers with bold yellow stamens.

Torenia fournieri 'Blue Moon', a wishbone flower, is also grown as summer bedding or a house plant.

Sutera 'Knysna Hills', the purple glory plant, with its spreading to semi-trailing stems and free-flowering habit, is ideal for softening hard edges.

Petunia Surfinia Series are ideal for hanging baskets because they have a markedly trailing habit and the blooms are long-lasting, produced in abundance over a long season, and remarkably weather-resistant. A similar effect can be created with ivy-leaved pelargoniums.

MORE CHOICES

HANGING BASKETS
Bidens ferulifolia
Diascia (trailing types)
Impatiens walleriana
Lobelia erinus (trailing cultivars especially)
Verbena

WINDOWBOXES
Capsicum annuum
Erysimum cheiri
Felicia amelloides
Impatiens hawkeri; New Guinea Group
Nolana humifusa
Pelargonium (trailing and ivy-leaved types)
Petunia
Sanvitalia procumbens
Scaevola aemula
Senecio cineraria

Brachyscome iberidifolia, or Swan River daisy, is a delightful, spreading to half-trailing annual with finely dissected foliage and myriad small daisies, each with a soft yellow centre.

Begonia semperflorens is a succulent, bushy annual with "sugared" flowers in shades of pink, red, purple, or white from summer to autumn.

Impatiens walleriana is the African busy Lizzie. It thrives in sun or part-shade and is one of the very best container plants. This Tempo Series has flowers in a range of colours, except true blue and yellow.

Verbena 'Tapien Pink' is a spreading plant with feathery leaves and flat clusters of rich pink flowers. It is free-flowering over a long season.

LOOKING AFTER YOUR PLANTS

THE KEY TO SUCCESS

A NNUALS AND BIENNIALS are generally rather undemanding plants, but to get the most out of them planting and care are important. It is well worth spending time on preparing the soil before sowing or planting, and choosing appropriate plants for the soil type and site. You will be rewarded with a succession of vigorous flowers from late spring through to autumn.

PREPARING THE GROUND

A border full of colourful annuals is an exciting and gratifying sight in any garden. To achieve this is not difficult, as long as the site is appropriate to the plants, the soil is well prepared, and the plants are healthy. Select an open, sunny site, preferably away from overhanging trees, with soil that is not too rich – most annuals thrive in average, well-drained soil. Soil preparation is best tackled in autumn, and completed over a few days so the task is less onerous.

SOIL PREPARATION

• Clean the area of pernicious weeds, such as bindweed or couch grass, if necessary, by applying systemic weedkillers.
• If the soil is in good condition, fork it over. If the soil is compacted, dig it over to a depth of a spade's blade.
• Remove all pieces of weeds, then rake level.
• Add a slow-release fertilizer to poor soils.
• Inspect the site regularly and weed if needed.

Sturdy, bushy growth

Unbalanced growth

BUYING A PLANT
When buying young plants for bedding, take care to choose vigorous, healthy plants with good, deep green foliage and no sign of pests or disease. Avoid any plants with yellowing leaves, stunted growth, dry, weedy compost, or pot-bound roots – they almost never thrive or flower well.

HEALTHY PLANT

UNHEALTHY PLANT

◀ PERFECT PARTNERS *Tall, spiky foxgloves soar above the large, crimson bowls of opium poppies.*

SOWING ANNUAL SEED UNDER COVER

R AISING PLANTS FROM SEED to flowering can be one of the most rewarding experiences in gardening. Annuals are ideal for the new or impatient gardener who wants quick and colourful results, because they often mature and flower within weeks of sowing. In temperate climates, seeds of most half-hardy and tender annuals are best sown under cover, so that the seedlings may be planted out once all danger of frost has passed.

SOWING INTO TRAYS

Standard or half seed trays are good for sowing fairly large quantities of seed. Always use clean containers and fresh, sterilized seed compost to avoid disease contamination. If the compost is too coarse, sieve it first to get a finely textured surface on which to sow. Once the seed is sown, the ideal place for them is in a greenhouse or cold frame, but a bright windowsill is fine, if it is out of direct sun.

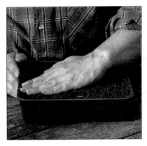

1 **Firm the compost** in the tray with another tray, a wooden presser, or your hand, to 1cm (½in) below the rim. Water well; allow to drain.

2 **Sow seed thinly** over the entire surface and, if the seeds are large, add a thin layer of seed compost to cover them. Label the tray.

3 **Cover the tray** with plastic film or glass to keep the compost moist. Put in a light place, not in full sun. Uncover when the seeds germinate.

SOWING INTO POTS

For smaller amounts of seed, you can use clay, plastic, or degradable pots. The method of sowing is the same as with trays (*see above*). Do not over-firm the compost or sow too thickly: this will result in crowded, spindly seedlings and runs the risk of fungal infection, which can quickly kill an entire potful. Always remember to label each pot to avoid confusion later.

USING VERMICULITE
Covering seed with a thin layer of vermiculite or fine grit keeps the seeds moist and protects them when watered.

Space large seeds evenly

DEGRADABLE POT
Sow 2 or 3 large seeds in a degradable pot. Thin to one seedling. Plant out in the pot to avoid disturbing the roots.

LOOKING AFTER SEEDLINGS

To develop healthily, seedlings need bright light and moisture. Light-starved seedlings (*see right*) rarely make vigorous plants, but they can also become scorched in strong sunlight. They must also never be allowed to dry out. If the compost is free-draining, over-watering should not be a problem.

Do not let seedlings linger too long in seed containers because they will become too crowded and develop extensive root systems that will be difficult to untangle when they are transplanted (*below*). The best time to transplant is when they have one or two true leaves; these develop after the first two leaves, which are seed leaves.

Long, drawn stems

PROVIDING LIGHT
Once seeds have germinated, it is important to ensure that the seedlings receive even, bright light. If not, they will become pale and drawn (etiolated). Turn containers on windowsills around regularly so that the seedlings are not drawn to one side.

1 **Lift seedlings carefully** from the compost using a widger or a pencil. Hold each seedling by its tiny leaves; if the fragile stem is damaged, the seedling will probably die.

2 **Insert the seedlings** in containers of fresh potting compost, spacing them evenly in rows and making a hole large enough to take each seedling's roots. Water with a fine spray.

USING MODULE TRAYS

Module trays come in many sizes and a variety of materials, but particularly plastic and polystyrene. They have an advantage over traditional trays and pots in that seedlings are disturbed as little as possible, each developing in its own compartment until it is ready to be potted up or planted out. Seed can be sown direct into small modules, or seedlings can be transplanted into larger modules. Modules can dry out quickly, so take care with watering.

SEEDLING PLUG PLANT
It is easy to keep the root ball of a seedling intact when lifting it from a module.

SOWING ANNUAL SEED OUTDOORS

MOST ANNUALS, ESPECIALLY HARDY AND HALF-HARDY kinds, are ideal for direct sowing outdoors. With little effort, large areas can be sown to create a riot of colour in a short time. Any decent, well-drained soil is fine, but soil preparation (*see p.45*) is the key to achieving a good display. Do not use fertilizers or organic manures – they make annuals too soft, lanky, and leafy – but add an organic fertilizer if annuals have been sown in the area before.

SOWING SEED BROADCAST

Scattering seed is quicker than sowing it in drills (*see facing page*), but has the disadvantage of not allowing any hoeing between rows of seedlings or young plants. To broadcast seed, rake the prepared ground to a fine tilth. Scatter the seed as evenly as possible, then lightly rake over the sown area to cover the seed.

SOWING THE SEED

COVERING THE SEED

MARKING OUT ANNUAL BORDERS

Annuals are most effective when sown in large blocks. To achieve this, mark out the ground, once it has been prepared and raked, by using pegs and strings, scouring the ground with a cane, or pouring lines of sand. Make each plot within the border fairly large; broad, overlapping sweeps are more effective than small, discreet ones.

MARKING OUT THE GROUND
Trickle lines of sharp sand or pour it from a bottle; it is easily seen and "rubbed out". Draw out one large area for each type of seed.

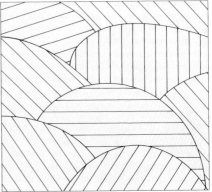

PLAN OF A PLOT FOR SOWING
Drills in adjacent plots should run in different directions. Mark them out with a cane or the point of a hoe, 10–12cm (4–5in) apart.

SOWING INTO DRILLS IN BORDERS

It helps to have made a rough plan on paper before starting to sow into the marked plots, so that you sow annuals of complementary heights and colours in adjacent blocks. The names of each annual can also be written on the plan for future reference. If the soil is very dry, water the drills lightly before sowing. Old annual seed can be sown more thickly than usual, because it tends to germinate erratically.

1 **Trickle the seeds** evenly and thinly from your hand along the bottom of the drill. Very fine seed can be sown direct from the packet. Try not to sow the seed too thickly.

2 **Cover the seed** by carefully brushing the soil across the drill. Firm the soil gently and water the drill using a watering can with a fine rose to avoid disturbing the seed.

3 **When the seedlings first appear,** they may look rather sparse, but they will soon fill in to form dense drifts. Check the rows regularly; hoe off any weeds between them.

4 **Thin the seedlings,** if necessary, to 5–6cm (2–2½in) apart, or more for large annuals. Pull out unwanted seedlings while firming the soil around those that are to be kept.

SOWING SEEDS SINGLY

Climbers such as morning glories, as well as annuals such as sunflowers, have fairly large seeds that can be sown individually. Make small holes in the prepared soil with your finger or a dibber and place one or two seeds in each, then cover with soil. The advantage of double sowing is that if one seed should fail, the other may germinate. If both seeds germinate, remove the weaker seedling. When sowing climbing annuals, place the supports, such as pea sticks or an obelisk, in position before sowing the seed.

SOWING SWEET PEAS BY A CANE WIGWAM
Sow two seeds at the base of each cane; thin out the weaker seedling at the 4-leaf stage.

PLANTING ANNUALS

ANNUALS RAISED IN SEED TRAYS, POTS, OR MODULES will need to be transplanted into the garden or containers. For hardy annuals, any time in spring will do, but for other types, it is best to wait until all danger of frost has receded; this may not be until early summer in some areas. In such cases, keep the new plants growing strongly by potting them on regularly in fresh compost.

PLANTING NEW ANNUALS IN A BED

As for seed sowing, it is crucial to prepare the soil (*see p.45*) before planting annuals. Ideally, the soil should be warm and moist, especially for the tender bedding annuals. Avoid planting into cold or very wet soils. Remove young plants from their containers with care, to avoid damaging their delicate root systems, and plant out evenly spaced.

PLANTING OUT MARIGOLDS

PLANTING A WINDOWBOX

A windowbox brings the garden almost into the house. Never be afraid to put in plenty of plants; sparsely planted containers look decidedly lack-lustre. Before planting, water the plants well and decide how to arrange them. Contrast bold annuals with dainty ones, erect plants with trailing types. Fill the windowbox with moist potting compost to within 2cm (¾in) of the rim; water-retentive granules can be added to the compost to keep it moist. Feed the planted windowbox regularly with liquid feed to keep the plants growing healthily.

1 **Knock each plant** gently from its pot, supporting the root ball at the base of the stem. Tease out the roots a little.

2 **Plant the larger, bolder** subjects first, so that the necks of the plants are 1cm (½in) below the rim, to allow for watering.

3 **Finish with trailing plants** at the front, firming each in gently. If needed, add more compost; level the surface, and water well.

PLANTING A HANGING BASKET

Generally, a mixture of bushy and trailing annuals works well in a hanging basket, although they can be effective if planted up with only one star performer, such as busy Lizzies. Once planted, baskets should be left for a few weeks under glass to establish before being placed on display outdoors, especially if tender annuals are used. The best site for a basket is in a warm part of the garden, sheltered from drying winds.

A PLANTED BASKET
Plant trailing and spreading annuals up the sides and around the edge, and bushy, upright ones in the centre, to form a globe of bloom.

BASKET LINERS

Baskets, whether plastic or metal, need to be lined to hold the compost and conserve water. Many people choose not to use the traditional lining material, sphagnum moss, since natural stocks are becoming exhausted. Modern materials include foam, felt, and coir liners. Some are pre-cut to the correct basket shape and size. Additional moisture retention can be gained by mixing water-retentive granules into the compost. Do not add too many, otherwise the compost will expand out of the basket like an over-risen cake.

FOAM LINER

1 **Support the basket** on a large pot. Press the liner into the basket and trim off any excess. Fill the lower third of the basket with potting compost and water-retentive granules.

2 **Cut cross slits** in the side of the liner with a sharp knife, to allow plants to be pushed through the liner, roots first. If moss is used, holes can be pushed through with the fingers.

3 **Ease trailing plants** through the slits, trying not to damage the roots unduly. Fill in the basket with more compost, plant up the top of the basket, firm gently, and water well.

BIENNIALS

SOME OF THE LOVELIEST HERBS grown in our gardens are biennials, that is, plants that flower in their second year from seed, then die, having first set seed. Biennials are rather awkward plants, taking up precious space for their first year without producing any flowers. However, many have interesting leaf-rosettes and sit comfortably in a mixed border or cottage garden, rather than a traditional annual border which is cleared at the end of the season.

GROWING ON BIENNIALS

Biennial seed may be sown in late winter or any time up to early summer. Many can be raised under glass and treated like bedding annuals, for planting out in early summer where they are to flower. A better option is to set aside a small plot for the biennials so that they do not need to be transplanted into their flowering positions until autumn; a part of the vegetable garden is ideal.

Sow biennials in a prepared seedbed in late spring or early summer, then transplant them into a nursery bed until autumn (*see below*). Alternatively, sow seed sparingly in drills at the nursery-bed spacings, thin the seedlings, and grow on. Place netting over them to keep off birds and cats (*see p.54*) and keep them watered. When seedlings emerge, protect them from slugs and snails.

CHOICE BIENNIALS

These biennials are all fully hardy and most are easy to raise from seed.

Bellis perennis, daisy
Campanula medium, Canterbury bell
Digitalis purpurea, foxglove
Eryngium giganteum, Miss Wilmott's ghost
Erysimum cheiri, wallflower
Lunaria annua, honesty
Meconopsis betonicifolia, Himalayan poppy (tricky to raise from seed)
Myosotis sylvatica, forget-me-not
Oenothera biennis, evening primrose
Onorpordum acanthium, Scotch thistle
Smyrnium perfoliatum, perfoliate Alexander
Verbascum bombyciferum, Turkish mullein

1 **As soon as the seedlings** are 5–8cm (2–3in) tall, in early summer, lift them from the seedbed using a hand fork. Retain as much soil around the roots as possible.

2 **Plant out** the seedlings 15–20cm (6–8in) apart, in rows 20–30cm (8–12in) apart, in a nursery bed. Allow the roots plenty of room. Firm in gently and water thoroughly.

3 **In the autumn,** lift the young plants and transfer them to their final positions. (If the nursery bed is dry, water it well several hours before digging up the plants.)

OVERWINTERING BIENNIALS

Most biennials are perfectly hardy. However, a few dislike excessive winter wet and are best protected by a plastic or glass cloche. Both Himalayan poppies and Turkish mulleins fall into this category. Whereas most biennials remain evergreen through the winter, often forming a symmetrical leaf-rosette, some, like the Himalayan poppy, wither back to an overwintering bud. A few, like the wallflower, make a bushy plant, even in the first year.

FIRST-YEAR SEEDLINGS
The leaf-rosettes of the Canterbury bell are evergreen, and send up flowering stems only in the spring of the second year.

Transplanting Self-sown Seedlings

Many biennials produce quantities of seed and will self-sow readily about the garden. Seedlings are often found in the vicinity of the parent plants, although sometimes the seed is blown considerable distances. It is not always easy to distinguish very small, biennial seedlings from those of weeds, so if you want to preserve the biennials, do not weed until all the seedlings have several true, or typical, leaves. You should then be able to recognize them and can either lift and transplant them to other parts of the garden (*see below*), or weed around them, leaving them to replace the parent plants.

1 **In late summer** or early autumn, look for seedlings nestling on the ground close to a mature plant (here a foxglove, *Digitalis purpurea*). Water the ground if it is dry.

2 **Lift the seedlings** gently using a trowel or a hand fork, being careful to keep as much soil as possible around the delicate roots to ensure the seedlings re-establish well.

3 **Replant the seedlings**, at least 30cm (12in) apart, where the plants are to flower the following year. Firm in gently and keep well watered until they are established.

PLANT CARE THROUGH THE SEASON

S EVERAL MEASURES CAN BE TAKEN to ensure even and healthy growth in young
annuals and biennials, and to achieve a better crop of bloom. Plants should
be protected from competing weeds and damaging pests, and given support if
necessary. Water only if the weather becomes too dry. Annuals in containers can
be fed by adding slow-release fertilizer to the compost or with liquid feeds, but
those in borders do not need feeding unless the soil is very impoverished.

PROTECTION AND SUPPORT

Half-hardy and tender plants raised under
cover need to be acclimatized, or hardened
off, for a few weeks before being planted in
the open garden. Protection from pests is
needed for vulnerable young plants. Tall or
climbing annuals and biennials and those
with thin stems benefit from some support,
from pea sticks or cylinders of wire mesh
to trellis. Whatever you use, put it in place
when the plants are young; it is harder to
do inconspicuously with semi-mature
plants, especially without damaging them.

HARDENING OFF YOUNG PLANTS
*Before planting out tender and half-hardy
annuals, acclimatize them by protecting them
from cold winds or frost with plastic or fleece.*

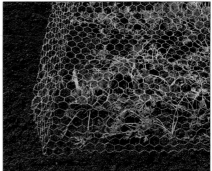

PROTECTION AGAINST PESTS
*Wire or plastic netting placed over young
plants will protect them from cats and birds.
Slug and snail controls may also be necessary.*

PROVIDING SUPPORT
*Pea sticks are ideal for annuals, disappearing
from sight as the plants grow. Place around
young plants, but not too close to their roots.*

TYING IN SUPPORTS
*Support tall annuals,
in containers or in
borders, by pushing
canes into the soil
and twining string
around the canes (see
left). Climbing plants
may need to be
started off by tying in
the shoots loosely –
with soft ties that
will not damage the
young growth.*

DEADHEADING

Regular deadheading removes unsightly fading blooms but, more importantly, prolongs the flowering season of many annuals and biennials. This is because plants divert energy from flowering to producing fruits, and cease flowering once they have developed mature seedheads. Large flowers are easiest to deadhead, but it is totally impractical to deadhead those with tiny flowers, such as gypsophila. If ornamental fruits or seed are required, then deadhead plants only lightly or not at all.

▲ SHORT-STEMMED FLOWERS
When each flower (here a petunia) fades, pinch off the stem with your fingers, close to the leaf joint below.

◀ FLOWERS WITH LONG STEMS
These are rather easier to deadhead: cut out the stems or flower spike (here of salvia) with secateurs or sharp scissors, but be sure to take out the stems close to the first mature leaves below, otherwise the deadheaded stalks will look unsightly and can allow disease to enter the plant.

END-OF-SEASON TASKS

During the autumn, particularly after the first frosts, annuals die down and look unsightly. At this stage, they are best pulled up and disposed off, either on the compost heap or burned; if seeding is likely to be a problem, then the latter option is the best. The soil can then be forked or dug over and well-rotted garden compost or bone meal worked in at the same time. Annuals can be grown successfully on the same plot of land for many years, provided it does not become infested with perennial weeds.

CLEARING DEAD AND DYING PLANTS
Use a rake to clear the ground methodically from the front of a border to the back. Try to avoid trampling on and compacting the soil, especially if it is quite heavy, such as clay.

WATERING TIPS

• Some annuals and biennials, especially busy Lizzies and petunias, need ample and regular watering throughout the summer. However, most need watering only in hot, dry weather.
• Overwatering causes lush, soft growth that is prone to flop over in wind or heavy rain. Plenty of water applied infrequently is far better than watering little and often.
• Always apply a fine, light spray over beds to avoid battering down plants; it is easier to water containers without wetting the plants.
• If possible, use rainwater or recycled water ("grey water", usually from the kitchen or bathroom) to conserve supplies. Do not use water that has added detergents.

COLLECTING SEED

Harvesting your own seed can be rewarding – and reduce your seed costs. Annuals and biennials often set seed in abundance, so you can share the seed with other gardeners. Many seeds come true to type, producing seedlings identical to the parent. Seed of hybrids and some named cultivars does not come true and plants are often inferior; such seed is best discarded. Some annuals, however, naturally hybridize and may give rise to pleasing variations.

EXTRACTING THE SEED

Seed is contained in many types of fruit or seedhead. In the simplest forms, seed is borne in a dry capsule; it can be shaken out or the capsule gently crushed to collect the seed. Some seedheads will fall apart into single-seeded pieces. In the flowerheads of daisies, numerous seeds are embedded in a flattened or cone-shaped disc, and these can be removed fairly readily. The most difficult fruits are those that are sticky or fleshy; it can be quite difficult and messy, and time-consuming, to extract the seed.

POPPIES
When the poppy seed capsule is mature, a ring of pores appears at the top and the tiny seeds can be shaken out, like pepper from a pepper pot. Shake the seed into paper packets.

GRASSES
Grass seed is ripe when the flowerheads begin to break up. Pull the head through your hand to sift seed and chaff into a collecting bag. After cleaning it, store seed in a paper bag.

SUNFLOWERS
The seedhead consists of hundreds of seeds partly embedded on the central disc. When the sunflower is dry and brown, the seeds are ripe. Rub them off by hand over clean paper.

HONESTY
Honesty seed pods are flat and oval, with the seeds pressed to a central membrane. Gently peel away the outer husks from each side of the membrane to expose the flat seeds.

PREPARING AND STORING SEED

Remember that seeds are live and they must be looked after carefully if they are to remain viable until the next year and achieve a good rate of germination. Home-collected seed should therefore be properly dried, sorted, and stored.

Ripe fruits or seedheads should be completely dry before they are stored, to avoid mould infecting and killing the seed. Often there will be some (or a great deal of) chaff or detritus mixed in with the seed and this will need to be separated out before the seed is stored. Papery seed capsules generally require little preparation and can be stored whole. The seed of fleshy fruits must be removed before the fruits start to rot and become mouldy, by picking individual seeds out by hand. Wear gloves when preparing seeds as some can cause skin allergies and others are poisonous.

Always store seed in paper packets or boxes; plastic bags increase humidity and the seed may rot. Make sure that the bags are clearly labelled, otherwise muddles are certain to occur, however well you think you can distinguish different seeds.

DRYING SEEDS
After collecting fruits and seedheads, place them in open boxes or paper bags. Leave for a day or so in a warm, dry place away from bright light and shake them occasionally.

SORTING SEEDS FROM CHAFF
Sieves of varying mesh size can be used to rid seed of unwanted chaff. Place the seed in the sieve and shake gently; if the sieve is the right size, only the seed will fall through.

STORING SEEDS
Place clean seed in paper envelopes or packets and label clearly. Store in a cool, dry place away from bright light, such as an airtight container on the lower shelf of a refrigerator.

PRACTICAL TIPS

• Most capsules are ripe when papery and brown; fleshy fruits when they change colour. Once plants have flowered, check regularly and collect seed as soon as they are ripe.

• Reject any fruits or seedheads that show signs of mould or other disease.

• Fine chaff can be sown with seed for garden use.

• Label each seed packet with the full plant name and date of collecting.

• Seed of many annuals and biennials can be stored at 1–5°C (34–41°F) for several years.

POT MARIGOLD

AVOIDING PLANT PROBLEMS

Annuals and biennials are, on the whole, remarkably free of pests and diseases in the garden, although young plants may be vulnerable to slugs and snails. Good garden hygiene, and vigorous plants that are grown in good soil and kept well watered, are more likely to remain healthy and free of pests or diseases. If problems do arise, there is generally no need to resort to noxious chemicals, which often kill indiscriminately, both friend and foe, in the garden.

PREVENTION AND CURE

Encouraging wildlife into the garden keeps many pests at bay, or at least at a level that causes no harm. Some annuals attract beneficial insects, so helping to protect more vulnerable plants such as roses. Birds seek out many insect pests, and it is easy to protect seedbeds or young plants from their foraging by placing netting or black cotton thread over the plants.

Cats can be troublesome, but a variety of devices, including ultrasound alarms and scented pellets, are available. The main pests in the garden are likely to be aphids and slugs or snails and various eco-friendly controls are commonly available.

More problems are likely to occur under glass, especially with the raising of half-hardy and tender annuals. Here scrupulous hygiene is crucial. Always use clean pots or trays and fresh, sterile compost. Red spider mite (*see below*) and vine weevils can be controlled biologically by releasing natural predators into the greenhouse.

Regularly inspect your plants, both in the garden and under glass, to spot problems at an early stage, when control is easier. Many pests can be picked off by hand. Once they are established, pests and diseases are more difficult to control and may already have inflicted considerable damage to the plants.

▲ RED SPIDER MITE DAMAGE
These mites are tiny, so the first sign is often brown speckling, then yellowing, of leaves. A humid atmosphere helps to keep mites at bay.

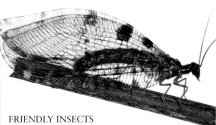

FRIENDLY INSECTS
The larvae of lacewings (above) *ladybirds* (right), *and dragonflies are particularly effective at keeping down aphids, one of the more troublesome garden pests. Rather than using any chemical pesticides, encourage these beneficial insects into the garden by using annuals and biennials rich in nectar.*

▶ DAMPING OFF
This fungal disease causes seedlings to collapse suddenly. Avoid it by sowing seed thinly, using sterile, free-draining compost in a clean container, and not overwatering the pot.

A CALENDAR OF SEASONAL REMINDERS

WINTER

• Tidy up annual beds, removing dead and dying growth for composting or burning. Take care not to add seedheads to compost heaps because they may germinate where they are not wanted the following year.

• Fork or dig over annual beds (or plots in mixed borders), leaving them bare during the winter so that the frosts can break down the soil and produce a fine surface by spring.

• Avoid trampling heavier soils, such as clay, especially in wet weather.

• Add bone meal or another slow-release, organic fertilizer to enrich the soil.

• Start planning and selecting annuals for the following year; browse in garden centres and seed catalogues before ordering seeds or plants for the spring.

• Draw up sowing or planting plans on paper, thinking about colour, height, and form, for the following season.

SPRING

• Start sowing tender and half-hardy annuals under glass in gentle heat.

• Sow seed of biennials outdoors, and more hardy annuals as gap-fillers in mixed borders.

• Outside, clear away any weeds that have appeared, and rake over the ground to level it and to produce a fine tilth.

• Start to sow seed of hardy annuals and biennials outdoors.

• Prick out half-hardy and tender annuals under glass, so they are frost-free.

• Thin hardy annuals if necessary.

• Check regularly for any signs of pests or diseases; protect new plants from slugs and snails and remove any plants that show signs of pests or disease.

• Commence staking tall or climbing annuals, eg.with canes, pea sticks, wire netting.

• Begin planting up containers for summer displays; grow on in a frost-free place.

USING CLOCHES
Annuals and biennials that have been direct-sown in the garden can be protected from cold and spring frosts under a cloche until conditions improve.

SUMMER

• Harden off half-hardy and tender plants once frosts have ceased.

• Finish staking annuals, being careful not to damage the young growth.

• Plant out half-hardy and tender annuals in the garden and in containers.

• Feed containers once the plants have become established, if the compost does not contain a long-term fertilizer.

• Water containers daily and young plants in dry periods.

• Weed regularly and inspect plants for signs of pests or diseases; control problems if needed.

• Regular, frequent deadheading will help to prolong the flowering season. If seed is required, stop deadheading while there are still a good number of flowering stems left at the end of the season.

• Start collecting seed as soon as the fruits and seed pods ripen; always clean, sort, and label all the collected seed promptly to ensure it is not confused with other seed later on.

• Commence sowing seed of half-hardy and tender annuals in nursery beds to grow on under cover for a winter display under cover.

AUTUMN

• Continue sowing seed of annuals under cover for a display in late winter and early spring.

• Transplant first-year biennials from their nursery beds to their flowering positions in the open garden. Plant in groups for the most effective display.

STRAWFLOWER SEEDHEAD

• Continue to collect seed as the fruits and seedheads ripen.

• Start to clear annual plants in containers as they finish flowering.

• Preserve any short-lived perennials used as bedding plants; plants such as pelargoniums and busy Lizzies can be potted up and over-wintered in a frost-proof greenhouse or in the house. Alternatively, take stem-tip cuttings.

• Clean, dry, and package seeds for storing over winter, preferably in the refrigerator; remember to label them clearly.

• Order some seed catalogues to prepare for the following year's display.

CHOICE ANNUALS AND BIENNIALS

THERE IS A VERY WIDE RANGE of annuals available to the gardener, both as seed and as young plants. The majority are undemanding, given a well-drained, sunny position, and many are fully hardy, needing no protection from frost. Plants are summer-flowering unless otherwise stated.

☼ *Prefers full sun* ☼ *Prefers partial shade* ❄ *Dislikes transplanting* ◊ *Prefers well-drained soil* ◊ *Prefers moist soil* ❋❋❋ *Fully hardy (down to −20°C/5°F)* ❋❋ *Frost-hardy (down to −5°C/23°F)* ❋ *Half-hardy (down to 0°C/32°F)* **Small** *Up to 30cm (12in)* **Medium** *30–90cm (12–36in)* **Tall** *Over 90cm (36in)* ♥ *RHS Award of Garden Merit*

A

Ageratum houstonianum (Floss flower)
Mound-forming, small to dwarf annual with oval leaves and masses of pink, blue, or white "powder-puff" flowers in summer to autumn. Good for butterflies. 'Blue Danube' ♥ is dwarf, with mid-sky-blue flowers; 'Bengali' has pale pink flowers that darken with age; 'White Cushion' is also good. Sow outdoors in late spring.
☼ ◊ ❋❋
'Adriatic' *p.36*

Agrostemma githago (Corn cockle)
Elegant, medium annual with paired, slender, pointed, grey-green leaves and pink, trumpet-blooms in summer. Good for annual meadows and cutting.
☼ ❄ ◊ ❋❋❋
'Milas' *p.30*

AGROSTEMMA GITHAGO
'MILAS'

Alcea rosea (Hollyhock)
Tall biennials or short-lived perennials, often grown as annuals, with large, rough, hand-shaped leaves and long spikes of broad, funnel-shaped, single or double flowers in a wide range of colours. 'Chater's Double' grows to 2.5m (8ft) and bears red, pink, yellow, or white, double flowers. 'Majorette' is 60cm (2ft) and 'Summer Carnival' is 2m (6ft), both with flowers in many colours. Sow under glass in the late summer or early spring.
☼ ◊ ❋❋❋

Amaranthus
Tall annuals with untoothed foliage and dense, feathery, or tassel-like clusters of tiny flowers during the summer. *A. hypochondriacus* has erect, broad or flattened heads of dark red flowers, and purple-flushed leaves, and is fully hardy, as is *A. caudatus* (love-lies-bleeding). *A. tricolor* (Chinese spinach) is a frost-hardy, bushy annual grown for its leaves in shades of red, crimson, or purple, often with contrasting gold, bronze, or rose. Sow outdoors in spring.
☼ ❄ ◊ Hardiness varies.
A. caudatus *p.37*

◄BRAZEN DAISIES *The brilliance of* Rudbeckia *'Radiant Gold' is softened by grasses in a border.*

Anchusa capensis (Alkanet)
Bushy, small to medium
biennial grown as an annual,
with bristly, lance-shaped
leaves and clusters of blue,
forget-me-not-like flowers.
Good for attracting butterflies
and bees. The medium 'Blue
Bird' produces sky-blue
flowers. Sow under glass in
summer or early spring.
☼ ◊ ❋❋
'Blue Angel' *p.30*

Anethum graveolens (Dill)
A popular, aromatic, medium,
annual herb (*p.22*) with finely
cut blue-green foliage and flat
heads of small, yellow-green
flowers. Good for cutting.
☼ ◊ ❋❋❋

Antirrhinum majus
(Snapdragon)
Small to medium perennial,
generally grown as an annual.
Bushy, with lance-shaped
leaves and spikes of fragrant,
pouched, two-lipped flowers
in a wide range of range of
colours as well as bicolours.
There are many selections,
from dwarf to tall, some with
open, bell-shaped flowers.

ANTIRRHINUM MAJUS
SONNET SERIES ♥

ARCTOTIS FASTUOSA 'ZULU
PRINCE'

Sonnet Series ♥ are medium
and free-flowering. Sow under
glass in early spring or late
summer or outside in spring.
☼ ◊ ❋❋

Arctotis fastuosa (Monarch
of the veldt)
A medium annual with deeply
lobed, elliptical, silvery leaves
and large, orange daisies with
dark markings at the petal
bases, and a blackish purple
disc, from midsummer until
autumn. 'Zulu Prince' has
white flowerheads and very
silver leaves. Harlequin
Hybrids (× *Venidioarctotis*)
have felty leaves and yellow,
orange, pink, white, apricot, or
red flowers. Good for cutting.
☼ ◊ min. 5°C/41°F

Argemone (Prickly poppy)
Robust, medium, prickly
plants with thistle-like leaves;
bears big, four-petalled poppy
flowers in summer, followed by
prickly seed pods. *A. mexicana*
has 8cm (3in) wide yellow or
orange flowers; *A. grandiflora*
has larger, white flowers. Sow
outside in spring.
☼ ❋ ◊ ❋

Atriplex hortensis
(Red mountain spinach,
Red orache)
Upright annual, to 1.2m (4ft),
with spinach-like foliage
in deep green to bronze or
purple-brown, or purple-red
in var. *rubra* (*p.6*). Bears long
clusters of tiny, reddish or
greenish brown flowers.
☼ ◊ ❋❋

B

Bassia scoparia f.
trichophylla ♥, syn. *Kochia
scoparia* (Burning bush)
Medium, bushy, fast-growing
annual, grown for its cypress-
shaped, linear foliage, which
turns deep red in autumn.
Sow under glass in spring.
☼ ◊ ❋❋

Begonia semperflorens
Small, bushy, fleshy perennials
grown for annual bedding.
The rounded, fairly brittle
leaves are dark green, bronze,
reddish or variegated. Plants
bear small clusters of single or
double flowers, in white, pink,
red, or apricot. Sow under
glass in early spring, or take
stem cuttings in summer and
early autumn.
☀ ◊ min. 13°C (55°F).
Begonia semperflorens *p.34,
p.43.* Also recommended:
Cocktail Series, 'Organdy'

Bellis perennis (Daisy)
A small, rosetted perennial
grown as a biennial, bearing
solitary, single, semi- or fully
double, button daisies above
the leaves on slender stalks.
Carpet Series and 'Goliath'
flowers are 8cm (3in) across,
'Pomponette' are 2.5cm (1in);
both come in pink, red, white,

Borago officinalis

or bicolours. Sow under glass in spring, outside in summer, or divide after flowering.

☼ ◊ ❀

Bidens ferulifolia ♥
Medium, spreading perennial grown as an annual, with finely cut foliage and bright yellow daisies. Good for containers. Sow under glass in early spring or take cuttings in summer and early autumn.

☼ ◊ ❀❀

Borago officinalis (Borage)
Medium to tall, bristly annual, sometimes overwintering, with large, oval leaves and clusters of nodding, star-shaped, blue or white flowers. Excellent bee flower. Sow seed in the spring; often self-seeds.

☼ ◊ ❀❀❀

Brachyscome iberidifolia
(Swan River daisy)
Small, spreading to trailing annual (*p.42*) or short-lived perennial with finely divided green leaves and small blue, pink, purple, or white daisies. Sow in early spring.

☼ ◊ ❀❀

Bracteantha bracteata syn.
Helichrysum bracteata
(Golden everlasting, Strawflower)
Small to medium, upright, branching annual (*p.17, p.31*) with lance-shaped leaves and large, papery daisies in many shades of red, yellow, orange, pink, and white, with yellow centres. Excellent for drying. Good butterfly plant. Dwarf to tall selections are available. Sow seed in spring.

☼ ☼ ◊ ❀

Brassica oleracea
(Ornamental brassicas)
Cabbages and kales grown for their colourful leaves; excellent autumn and winter bedding. Osaka Series make open, cabbage-like plants to 45cm (18in), with wavy, bluish green outer leaves and pink or red centres. 'Tokyo' is similar but grows to just 25cm (10in).

☼ ◊ ❀

Browallia speciosa
(Sapphire flower)
Medium, bushy perennial grown as an annual, with oval leaves and showy flowers in violet-blue with white centres, or white in the compact form 'White Troll'. Sow under glass in early spring.

☼ ◊ min. 10°C (50°F)

C

Calendula officinalis
(Pot or English marigold)
Bushy annuals and short-lived perennials with rough, aromatic, succulent, elliptical, pale green leaves and daisy-like, single or double flowers in yellow, orange, apricot, or cream. Good for cutting.

Callistephus chinensis
'Giant Princess'

Many selections are available in various sizes. Sow seed in spring; often self-seeds.

☼ ◊ ❀❀❀

Callistephus chinensis
(China aster)
Medium or small, bushy annuals with oval, toothed leaves. Many selections, dwarf and tall, with single, semi-, or fully-double, pompon or quilled daisies, in most hues except yellow. Tall types are good for cutting. Sow under glass in early spring.

☼ ◊ ❀❀

Campanula medium
(Canterbury bells)
A medium biennial forming a coarse, evergreen leaf-rosette in the first year. Bears large pyramids of bell-shaped, single or double flowers in shades of blue, purple, pink, or white in late spring to early summer. In 'Cup and Saucer' ♥, the calyx, normally green, is expanded, saucer-like, and coloured like the petals. Sow under glass, or in open ground in summer.

☼ ◊ ❀❀❀

C. isophylla 'Stella Blue' *p.4*

Capsicum annuum
(Chilli pepper)
Small, bushy plants with lance-shaped to elliptical, mid-green leaves and handsome, glossy fruits. The best ornamental peppers are the Cerasiforme Group (cherry pepper), with small, round fruits in purple, yellow, or red, and the Conoides Group (cone pepper), with upright, conical fruits in white, green, or scarlet.
☀ ◊ min. 5°C (41°F)

Celosia argentea
Medium, bushy perennial grown as an annual, with oval, mid-green leaves and pyramidal, feathery clusters of tiny flowers in yellow, apricot, pink, or red. In var. *cristata*, the flowers form a flattened head like a cock's-comb. Sow under glass in early spring.
☀ ◊ ✳✳

Centaurea cyanus
(Cornflower)
A small to medium, upright annual (*p.33*) with narrow, lance-shaped, grey-green leaves. In summer to autumn, bears numerous blue, purple, pink, or white daisy-like flowers. The species is good for naturalizing; cultivars of different heights are available. Excellent for cutting. Sow in autumn or early spring.
☀ ☀ ◊ ✳✳✳

Chrysanthemum carinatum
(Annual chrysanthemum)
Fast-growing, medium, bushy annual with feathery, fairly succulent, pale green foliage and large daisies in various hues, usually with rings of bold, contrasting colour in the centre. Good for cutting. Both

CLEOME HASSLERIANA
'ROSE QUEEN'

small and medium types are available, as well as single- and double-flowered forms. Sow seed in spring.
☀ ☀ ◊ ✳✳

Clarkia amoena syn.
Godetia amoena
An upright, medium annual with lance-shaped leaves and spikes of single or double flowers with satiny, often frilled petals in shades of pink, mauve, and scarlet. *C. pulchella* is taller, with smaller flowers in a similar colour range. Sow in spring.
☀ ☀ ◊ ✳✳✳

Cleome hassleriana syn.
C. spinosa (Spider plant)
Tall, stout annual with hairy stems and mid-green, handlike leaves. Bears broad clusters of strongly scented flowers with narrow pink, mauve, purple, or white petals and prominent stamens. Cultivars have showier flowers than the species. Sow seed under glass in early spring.
☀ ◊ ✳
'Helen Campbell' ♥ *p.15*. Also recommended: 'Rose Queen'

Consolida ajacis (Larkspur)
Tall, elegant annual with finely cut, feathery foliage and large spikes of single or double, spurred flowers in blue, pink, mauve, or white. Excellent for cutting and for drying. Cultivars of all heights are available. Sow in spring, or autumn in mild areas.
☀ ◊ ✳✳✳
Imperial Series *p.37*

Convolvulus tricolor
Upright to spreading annual with funnel flowers in blue, pink, or mauve, with white and yellow centres, opening in sun. Sow seed in spring.
☀ ◊ ✳✳✳
'Royal Ensign' *p.31*. Also recommended: 'Blue Flash'

Coreopsis (Tickseed)
Medium, bushy plants with green, lance-shaped leaves and bright yellow daisies in summer to early autumn. *C. tinctoria* is an annual; *C. grandiflora*, a perennial often grown as an annual, has buttercup-yellow flowers. Good for cutting.
☀ ◊ ✳✳✳

COREOPSIS TINCTORIA

RECOMMENDED CLIMBERS

Cardiospermum halicacabum (Balloon vine)
A fairly tall – to 3m (10ft) – tendrilled, deciduous climber often grown as an annual. Slender stems bear attractive two-lobed leaves and inconspicuous flowers, followed in summer and autumn by lantern-like, straw-coloured seed capsules. Sow seed under glass in spring.
☼ ◊ min. 5°C (41°F).

Cobaea scandens ♀
(Cup-and-saucer vine) Rampant, tendrilled climber with deep green leaves and solitary, bell-shaped flowers that are green when they open and age to purple, or to white in f. *alba* ♀. Sow under glass in spring.
☼ ◊ min. 5°C (41°F)

Eccremocarpus scaber ♀
(Chilean glory vine) Tendrilled evergreen, to 4m (12ft), grown as an annual but often overwintering. Has dissected, grey-green leaves and long-stalked clusters of tubular flowers in red, orange or pink, followed by pendent, lemon-shaped, inflated seed pods.
☼ ◊ ✽✽

Ipomoea (Morning glory)
Twining climbers with heart-shaped leaves and funnel-shaped flowers, opening in sun. *I. alba* (Moon flower, min. 10°C/50°F), is an evergreen to 7m (22ft), with large (15cm/6in), fragrant

LABLAB PURPUREUS

white flowers. The common morning glory, *I. purpurea* (min. 5°C/41°F), to 4m (12ft), has white, blue, purple or reddish flowers. I. tricolor needs a min. 5°C (41°F).
☼ ◊ min. varies
'Grandpa Ott' *p.15*, I. lobata *p.25*, I. tricolor 'Heavenly Blue' ♀ *p.33*

Lablab purpureus (Lablab)
Vigorous, twining, deciduous perennial grown as an annual, to 5m (15ft), with trefoil leaves and purple or pinkish pea flowers followed by showy, purple-red, shiny seed pods. Sow seed under glass in spring.
☼ ◊ min. 5°C (41°F).

Lathyrus odoratus
(Sweet pea) ♀
Annual (*p.24*) with winged stems to 3m (10ft). Bears long-stalked clusters of large, finely scented pea-flowers, in many colours except yellow. Many cultivars are available, mostly climbing. Ideal cut flower. Sow under glass in autumn or early spring.
☼ ◊ ✽✽✽

Rhodochiton atrosanguineus ♀
Twining perennial grown as an annual (*p.25*) to 3m (10ft), with heart-shaped leaves. Drooping, tubular, reddish-purple flowers in summer and autumn have hat-like, pinkish calyces.
☼ ◊ min. 3–5°C (37–41°F)

Thunbergia alata (Black-eyed Susan)
Twining annual (*p.40*) to 3m (10ft), with arrowhead-shaped leaves and showy, sideways-facing, trumpet flowers in orange, cream, yellow, or apricot and with black centres. Sow seed under glass in spring.
☼ ◊ ✽

Tropaeolum
T. majus (nasturtium) climbs to 3m (10ft), with spurred, trumpet flowers mainly in red, orange, yellow, and pink. *T. peregrinum*, to 2.5m (8ft), has yellow, bird-like flowers. Sow under glass in early spring, outside in late spring.
☼ ◊ min. 3°C (37°F)
T. peregrinum p.25

LATHYRUS ODORATUS 'MARS'

Cosmos bipinnatus
(Cosmea)
A branched annual to 1.5m
(5ft) with feathery foliage and
large, daisy-like flowers in
pink, mauve, red, and white.
Good for cutting. Modern
selections are often only 60cm
(2ft) tall. *C. sulphureus* has
golden flowers. Sow in spring.
☼ ◊ ❀❀❀

D

Dahlia
The smaller perennial bedding
or border dahlias grown as
annuals are bushy, 20–50cm
(8–20in) tall, with deep-green,
fleshy leaves and numerous
single, semi-, or fully double
flowers in many shades except
blue. Good for cutting. Many
selections are available. Sow
under glass in spring; take
cuttings or divide in spring.
☼ ◊ min. 5°C (41°F)
Recommended: 'Fascination'
♥, 'Sunny Yellow' ♥

Dianthus (Pink)
Small to medium, bushy plants
with lance-shaped to linear
leaves and fragrant, usually

DAHLIA COLTNESS HYBRID

DIANTHUS 'CHERRY PICOTEE'

fringed flowers, mostly in red,
pink, and white, often finely
marked, and a few yellows
like 'Bookham Fancy'. Good
for cutting. *D. barbatus* (sweet
William) has dense, flat flowerheads. *D. chinensis* (Chinese,
Indian pink) has deep-fringed,
single or double blooms. Sow
in spring or early summer.
☼ ◊ ❀❀❀
D. 'Telstar' *p.17*

Digitalis (Foxglove)
Softly downy biennial or
short-lived perennial, forming
a coarse, evergreen leaf-rosette
in the first year. Flowers are
tubular, purple, pink, yellow,
or white, often spotted
within, in dense, one-sided,
tapered spikes up to 1.2m
(4ft). Excellent for bees and
naturalizing. Sow in spring or
summer; often self-seeds.
☼ ◊ ❀❀❀
D. purpurea p.32, p.53

Dimorphotheca pluvialis
(Rain daisy)
Small, bushy annual (*p.30*)
with dark green, elliptical
leaves and large white daisies
with brownish purple centres,
opening in sun. Sow in spring.
☼ ◊ ❀

Dorotheanthus bellidiformis
(Livingstone daisy,
Mesembryanthemum)
Low, carpeting annual with
grey, "crystalline" leaves and
daisies in vivid shades of
yellow, red, pink, or white,
often with dark centres,
opening in sun. Sow seed in
early spring under glass.
☼ ◊ ❀

E

Echium vulgare
(Viper's bugloss)
Small to medium, bushy, bristly
annual or biennial with lance-
shaped leaves and spiralled
clusters of tubular flowers in
shades of purple, pink, blue,
or white. Dwarf forms are
available. Sow in spring.
☼ ◊ ❀❀❀

Eryngium giganteum ♥
(Miss Willmott's ghost)
Tall biennial with very prickly
leaves and thistle-like, blue
flowerheads and prominent,
holly-like, silvery bracts.
Excellent for drying. Sow in
spring; often self-seeds. (In the
first year, rosette is not spiny.)
☼ ◊ ❀❀❀

Erysimum cheiri
syn. *Cheiranthus cheiri*
(Wallflower)
A medium, bushy biennial or
short-lived perennial with deep-
green, elliptical leaves and
clusters of sweetly scented
flowers in red, yellow, orange,
bronze, and cream in spring.
Good for bedding with bulbs.
Many selections available,
including dwarf types. Sow
seed in early summer.
☼ ◊ ❀❀❀
'Fire King' *p.14*

EUPHORBIA MARGINATA

Eschscholzia californica ♀
(California poppy)
Small to medium, rather
succulent annual (*p.31*),
sometimes overwintering,
with grey- or blue-green, fern-like foliage. The four-petalled,
satiny flowers come in shades
of yellow, orange, red, pink,
and apricot, sometimes
bicoloured, and open in sun.
The many selections include
types with frilled and semi-double flowers. Sow in spring,
or in autumn in mild areas.
☼ ◊ ❋❋
E. lobbii p.32, 'Yellow Cap'
p.14

Euphorbia marginata
(Snow-on-the-mountain)
An upright, medium, bushy
annual, with elliptical, bright-green leaves. The numerous
attractive bracts surround
insignificant, greenish flowers.
Sow seed in spring.
☼ ◊ ❋❋❋

Exacum affine (Persian
violet)
Small, bushy annual (*p.42*)
with bright green, succulent,
oval leaves. Bears numerous
small flowers in blue, violet,
or purple in late spring and
summer. Good for containers.
Sow in late summer or spring.
◑ ◊ min. 5°C (41°F)

F

Felicia amelloides
(Blue daisy)
Small, bushy shrub grown as
an annual, with oval leaves
and yellow-centred, blue
daisies. Sow seed under glass
in early spring, or take stem
cuttings in summer.
☼ ◊ ❋

RECOMMENDED GRASSES

Briza maxima (Greater
quaking grass)
An upright, slender, medium
annual (*p.23, p.56*) with mid-green leaves, mainly at the
base, and sprays of nodding
purplish-green flowers. Very
good for drying. Sow in
spring; self-seeds readily.
☼ ◊ ❋❋❋

Hordeum jubatum
(Foxtail barley)
Medium, tufted annual or
short-lived perennial (*p.23*).
The feathery, arched plumes
are flushed pink, then straw-coloured. Sow in spring.
☼ ◊ ❋❋❋

Lagurus ovatus ♀ (Hare's-tail grass)
Small to medium, tufted
annual with pale-green
leaves and pointed, soft

white flowerheads with
yellow stamens. Good for
drying. Sow seed in spring.
☼ ◊ ❋❋❋

Pennisetum setaceum
(Fountain grass) ♀
A tall, tufted, perennial grass
that can be grown as an
annual, with rough, mid-green leaves and cylindrical

spikes of copper-red that
last well into winter. Sow
seed in spring.
☼ ◊ ❋❋

Setaria italica
(Foxtail millet)
Tall, tufted annual grass
with narrow, lance-shaped
leaves and lax heads of
white, cream, yellow, red,
brown, or black. Good for
drying. Sow in late spring.
☼ ❋ ◊ ❋

Zea mays ♀ (Maize,
Sweetcorn)
Medium to tall annual;
the tasselled female flowers
become corncobs. Some
cultivars have different
coloured or multi-coloured
cobs; good for drying. Sow
under glass in early spring.
☼ ◊ ❋

LAGURUS OVATUS

G

Gaillardia pulchella
(Blanket flower)
Medium, upright, bushy annual with grey-green, lance-shaped leaves and single to fully double daisies in yellow, red, pink, or crimson, often bicolored. Good for cutting. Sow seed in spring.
☼ ◊ ❀❀❀

Gazania
Low-growing perennials, often grown as annuals, with lance-shaped, leathery, deep-green to white-felted leaves and large daisies, often in bright yellow, orange, or red with darker central markings, sometimes cream, white, or pink. Sow seed in early spring.
☼ ◊ ❀
Daybreak Series ♥ *p.41.*
Also recommended: Talent Series ♥, Chansonette Series ♥.

Gilia
Medium annuals with feathery foliage and button flowerheads from summer to early autumn. *G. capitata* (Queen Anne's thimbles) has lavender-blue flowers. *G. tricolor* (bird's-eyes) has violet flowers with orange or yellow centres and purple spots. Sow in spring.
☼ ◊ ❀❀❀

Glaucium corniculatum
(Red horned poppy)
Medium biennial or short-lived perennial with oblong, lobed, silvery-grey leaves and orange, bowl-shaped flowers followed by long, curved seed pods. Similar, but with bluish leaves and dark orange to crimson flowers, is *G. grandiflorum.*
☼ ◊ ❀❀❀

Gomphrena globosa
(Globe amaranth)
Small, bushy annual with oval, hairy leaves and pink, purple, orange, yellow, or white, clover-like flowerheads. Good for cutting. Sow under glass or in open ground in spring.
☼ ◊ ❀

Gypsophila elegans
(Annual gypsophila)
A medium, upright, branched annual (*p.5*) with grey-green, lance-shaped leaves and spreading sprays of numerous small, white flowers. Excellent for cutting. Sow in spring.
☼ ❀ ◊ ❀❀❀

H

Helianthus annuus
(Sunflower)
A rough, hairy annual to 3m (10ft), with 1 erect stem, ace-of-spade leaves, and 20–40cm (8–16in) flowerheads with brown or purple discs (*p.56*). Some have double flowers, others smaller flowers and branched stems, dwarf forms are 30–50cm (12–20in) tall. Flowers range from cream, orange, and yellow to brown and rust. Good for cutting and drying. Sow in spring.
☼ ◊ ❀❀❀
H. 'Pastiche' *p.22*

HELIANTHUS 'GIANT SINGLE'

HELIOTROPIUM ARBORESCENS

Helichrysum petiolare ♥
Medium, spreading to trailing, evergreen shrub grown as an annual. The small, silver-grey, round to heart-shaped leaves are very attractive; the often sparse flowers, creamy yellow. Sow in spring or take semi-ripe cuttings in summer.
☼ ◊ ❀
'Variegatum' ♥ *p.19*

Heliophila coronopifolia
Low-growing to medium, rather slender annual with simple or lobed leaves and numerous small, blue, four-petalled flowers with yellow-green centres. Sow in spring.
☼ ❀ ◊ ❀❀

Heliotropium arborescens
(Cherry pie)
Bushy, evergreen shrub grown as an annual, with glossy deep-green, narrow, wrinkled leaves and dense, flat clusters of sweetly scented, lavender to purple flowers. Cultivars come in blue, purple, violet, and pink. Sow seed in spring, or take cuttings in summer and early autumn.
☼ ◊ ❀

Hibiscus

Annuals or short-lived perennials with lobed leaves and funnel-shaped flowers that open in sun. *H. acetosella* is tall, with yellow or purple-red flowers with deep purple centres. *H. trionum* (flower-of-the-hour) is medium with serrated leaves and cream or yellow flowers with purple-brown centres. Sow under glass in early spring.

☼ ◊ ✿✿

Hunnemannia fumariifolia

(Mexican tulip poppy) Short-lived perennial grown as an annual, with large, bright yellow flowers. It looks like *Eschscholzia* (*see p.67*), but has coarser leaves. Good for cutting. Sow in spring.

☼ ☼ ◊ ✿✿

I

Iberis umbellata (Candytuft)

Mound-forming annual with lance-shaped leaves and flat heads of uneven, pink, purple or white flowers, summer to early autumn. Sow in spring, or in autumn in mild areas.

☼ ☼ ◊ ✿✿✿

Impatiens (Balsam)

Succulent, small to medium annuals or perennials grown as annuals, with lance-shaped to elliptical, serrated leaves. Busy Lizzie (*I. walleriana*) is spreading, with long-spurred, flat flowers in hues of apricot, purple, pink, red, orange, and white. Good for containers and bedding; tolerates shade. *I. balsamina* (Indian balsam) is upright, with narrow, lance-shaped leaves and hooded, single or double, pink, red,

IMPATIENS NEW GUINEA GROUP

purple, mauve, or white flowers with short, hooked spurs. New Guinea Group are bushy and upright, with large leaves, often flushed bronze, red, or purple, and large, flat, spurred blooms in purple, pink, white, scarlet, orange, or apricot. Seed pods explode when ripe to expel the seed. Sow seed in early spring under glass or take cuttings in summer and autumn.

☼–☼ ◊ ✿ min. varies from 5–10°C (41–50°F)
Mixed hybrids *p.5, p.34, p.45,* **Super Elfin Series** ♀ *p.41,* **Tempo Series** ♀ *p.43*

L

Lantana camara

Scrambling, evergreen shrub, sometimes grown as an annual, with finely wrinkled, oval leaves and rounded heads of small, orange, yellow, purple, pink, red, and white flowers all summer. Flowers often open pale and darken to a different shade; those in the centre open last. There are many cultivars.

☼ ◊ ✿

Lavatera trimestris

Vigorous, tall, leafy annual (*p.33*) with heart-shaped, lobed leaves and large, satiny, funnel-shaped flowers in summer and early autumn. 'Silver Cup' has rose-pink flowers with deeper veins; 'Mont Blanc' has white flowers. Sow seed in spring.

☼ ◊ ✿✿✿
'Mont Blanc' *p.31*

Layia platyglossa

(Tidy tips) Fast-growing, small to medium annual with grey-green, lance-shaped leaves and abundant, small, daisy-like flowers in yellow, ringed with white. Excellent for butterflies and for cutting. Sow seed in early spring.

☼ ◊ ✿✿✿

Leucanthemum paludosum

A small, bushy annual (*p.35*) with oval to wedge-shaped, lobed or toothed leaves and small, solitary, yellow daisies with a darker centre. 'Show Star' has yellow-green foliage. Sow seed in spring.

☼ ◊ ✿✿✿

LEUCANTHEMUM PALUDOSUM 'SHOW STAR'

Limnanthes douglasii
(Poached-egg plant) ♀ ·
Small, spreading annual with
bright green, pinnate leaves
(*p.27*). It has egg-yolk yellow,
saucer-shaped flowers, usually
ringed with white, in late
spring to early summer. Sow
in autumn or spring; self-seeds.
☼ ◐ ❋❋❋

Limonium sinuatum (Sea
lavender, Statice)
Medium, erect perennial grown
as an annual (*p.20*), with a
basal rosette of dull-green,
wavy-edged, oblong leaves,
and branched spikes of everlasting, papery flowers in pink,
red, purple, mauve, yellow,
and white. Excellent for
drying; good for butterflies.
☼ ◊ ❋❋

Linaria maroccana
Small, bushy annual with pale
green, linear to lance-shaped
leaves and slender clusters of
small, two-lipped flowers in
pink, red, purple, yellow,
white, or bicolours, with a
pointed spur. Sow in spring.
☼ ◊ ❋❋❋

Linum grandiflorum
'Rubrum' (Flax)
Upright, small to medium
annual with lance-shaped
leaves and vivid saucer-shaped
flowers (*p.32*). Sow in spring.
☼ ☼ ◊ ❋❋❋

Lobelia erinus
Tufted or trailing annuals,
sometimes overwintering, with
oval to lance-shaped, green to
bronze or purple leaves and
many small, two-lipped
flowers in blue, pink, purple,
red, mauve, or white. Excellent
for bedding; trailing types are
also good for containers. Sow

under glass in early spring.
☼ ◐ ❋
'Cambridge Blue' ♀ *p.36*,
'Crystal Palace' ♀ *p.32*,
'Sapphire' *p.40*,
'Snowball' *p.32*

Lobularia maritima
(Sweet alyssum)
Small, tufted to mat-forming
annual with narrow, lance-
shaped, grey-green leaves, and
dense clusters of tiny, sweetly
scented flowers in pink, purple,
or white as in 'Little Dorrit'.
Excellent for edging. Many
cultivars available. Good
butterfly plant. Sow in spring.
☼ ◊ ❋❋❋
L. Easter Bonnet Series *p.26*

Lunaria annua (Honesty)
Biennial growing to 75cm
(30in), forming a lax rosette
of heart-shaped leaves in the
first year; produces branched
clusters of purple, scented,
four-petalled flowers in spring
and early summer, then flat,
silvery seed pods (*p.21*, *p.56*)
that are excellent for drying.
'Variegata' has paler flowers
and cream-variegated leaves.
☼ ◊ ❋❋❋

LOBULARIA MARITIMA
'LITTLE DORRIT'

Lupinus (Lupin)
Annual lupins are medium
to tall, with rounded, deeply
divided leaves and small, pea-
like flowers borne in dense,
tapering spikes. *L. hartwegii*
blooms are pale blue, *L. luteus*
bright yellow. Sow in spring.
☼ ☼ ◊ ❋❋

M

Malcolmia maritima
(Virginia stock)
Small, fast-growing annual
with grey-green leaves and
sparse clusters of dainty,
scented flowers in red, pink,
or white, spring and summer.
Sow in succession in spring
and early summer, or autumn.
☼ ◊ ❋❋❋

Malope trifida
(Annual mallow)
Tall annual with lobed leaves
and large, satiny, funnel-
shaped flowers in purple-red
with deeper veins. 'Vulcan'
has bright magenta-pink
flowers. Sow seed in spring.
☼ ◊ ❋❋❋

MALOPE TRIFIDA
'VULCAN'

MATTHIOLA INCANA
CINDERELLA SERIES

MENTZELIA LINDLEYI

Matthiola incana
(Brompton stock)
A medium, bushy biennial or short-lived perennial (p.26), with elliptical, grey leaves and sweetly scented, four-petalled flowers. 'Giant Excelsior' is tall, with pink, red, pale-blue, or white, double flowers. The shorter Cinderella Series also has dark blues. Ten Week Series is fast-growing, with single flowers in many shades. Sow under glass in spring.
☼ ◑ ❋❋❋

Meconopsis betonicifolia ♀
(Himalayan poppy)
Tall biennial or perennial with bristly leaves and large, open poppy flowers in violet, blue, or mauve, with yellow anthers. Needs lime-free soil.
◐ ◑ ❋❋❋

Mentzelia lindleyi
syn. *Bartonia aurea*
(Blazing star)
Fast growing, medium, bushy annual with fern-like leaves and bright yellow flowers with pointed petals. Good for cutting. Sow in spring.
☼ ❋ ◊ ❋❋❋

Mimulus (Monkey flower)
Succulent, spreading annuals or short-lived perennials with fresh-green, toothed, elliptical foliage. The flowers, like open snapdragons, are often spotted or blotched. *M. guttatus* has bright-yellow flowers with reddish-brown blotches. Sow seed under glass in spring.
☼ ◑ ❋❋❋
M. Malibu Series *p.41*

Mirabilis jalapa
(Marvel of Peru, Four o'clock flower)
Medium, bushy perennial, sometimes grown as an annual or biennial, with oval, mid-green leaves and long, trumpet-shaped flowers in magenta, red, pink, yellow, or white, often with several colours on the same plant, opening late in the afternoon.
◐ ◑ ❋❋

Moluccella laevis
(Bells of Ireland)
Medium, erect annual (p.14) with round, pale green leaves and small, white flowers, each backed by a conspicuous, green, persistent, collar-like calyx. Excellent for cutting and drying. Sow under glass or outdoors in late spring.
☼ ◊ ❋❋

Myosotis sylvatica
(Forget-me-not)
Small, tufted annual or biennial with elliptical, grey-green leaves and spirals of small, blue flowers in spring and summer. Many cultivars include ones with blue, violet, pink, or white flowers, and compact types for formal bedding. 'Music' is erect, with large, bright blue flowers. Sow in spring or summer.
☼ ◊ ❋❋❋

N

Nemesia strumosa
Small, bushy annual with lance-shaped, serrated leaves and two-lipped, funnel-shaped flowers in a range of bright colours. The compact forms such as Triumph Series are excellent for formal bedding.
☼ ◊ ❋
'Fragrant Cloud p.19,
N. versicolour 'Blue Bird' *p.14*

MYOSOTIS SYLVATICA
'MUSIC'

Nemophila menziesii
(Baby blue-eyes)
Small, delicate annual with
narrow, serrated, grey-green
leaves and small, saucer-
shaped, bright-blue flowers
with white centres.
☼ ◊ ❀❀❀
N. maculata *p.19*

Nicotiana (Tobacco plant)
Medium annual with
elliptical, sticky leaves and lax
clusters of long-throated, flat-
faced flowers in the summer
and autumn. *N. alata* has
white flowers, brownish violet
on the outside, opening and
strongly scented at evening.
N. × sanderae hybrids are
popular for bedding and for
containers, with a wide range
of colours, particularly green,
red, pink, purple and white,
the latter often scented. Sow
seed under glass in spring.
☼ ◊ ❀
N. 'Lime Green' ♥ *p.40*. Also
recommended: *N. langsdorfii* ♥

Nierembergia caerulea
syn. *N. hippomanica* ♥
Small, bushy perennial with
lance-shaped leaves and

bowl-shaped, five-lobed, blue,
violet, or purple flowers – or
white in 'Mont Blanc' – in
summer and early autumn.
Sow under glass in spring.
☼ ◊ ❀
Also recommended: 'Purple
Robe'

Nigella damascena
(Love-in-a-mist)
Medium, upright annual with
flat, multi-petalled flowers
backed by a ruff of feathery
leaves, and followed by
inflated seed capsules (*p.2*),
excellent for drying. Persian
Jewels Series has blue, pink,
or white flowers; 'Miss Jekyll'
♥ has rich blue flowers.
N. hispanica has unruffled
purple flowers and dark seed
capsules. Sow seed in autumn
or spring; often self-seeds.
☼ ❀ ◊ ❀❀❀
Persian Jewels Series *p.31*

O

Ocimum basilicum (Basil)
A small to medium, highly
aromatic culinary herb with
elliptical, shiny, deep-green

foliage and spikes of small,
two-lipped flowers in pink or
white. Many cultivars are
available, including some with
leaves in red, bronze, or
purple, as in 'Dark Opal', or
with ruffled edges. Sow seed
successively from late spring.
☼ ◊ ❀

Oenothera biennis
(Evening primrose)
A tall, stiff-stemmed biennial
with elliptical, grey-green
leaves and primrose-yellow,
scented funnel-flowers that
unfurl in the evening. Sow in
spring; often self-seeds.
☼ ◊ ❀❀❀

Onopordum acanthium
(Cotton or Scotch thistle)
An imposing, tall, extremely
prickly biennial, forming a
large, spiny-leaved rosette in
the first year, then growing to
1.8m (6ft). The stem is very
leafy, with spiny wings, and
branched above to carry
the relatively large, purple,
typical thistle flowerheads.
Good for drying. Sow seed in
spring or summer.
☼ ◊ ❀❀❀

NIEREMBERGIA CAERULEA
'MONT BLANC'

OCIMUM BASILICUM
'DARK OPAL'

OSTEOSPERMUM
'WHIRLIGIG'

PAPAVER SOMNIFERUM

PELARGONIUM HORIZON SERIES

PETUNIA CARPET SERIES

Osteospermum
Short to medium perennials, sometimes grown as annuals, with oval to elliptical leaves and showy daisies in white, yellow, purple, or pink, often with a contrasting central disc, in summer and autumn. Species include *O. ecklonis* (white with a dark blue disc), *O. fruticosum* (white with a purplish violet disc), and *O. jucundum* (mauve-pink to magenta with a purple disc). Some cultivars have crimped petals. Sow seed in spring.
☼ ◊ ❋❋ (borderline)

P

Papaver (Poppy)
Genus including annuals with lobed or divided leaves and showy, four-petalled flowers. *P. alpinum* (alpine poppy) is a small annual or short-lived perennial with grey-green foliage and small flowers in pink, white, yellow, orange, or apricot. *P. rhoeas* (corn poppy) has deep green leaves and red flowers with black centres. *P. commutatum* ♥ has scarlet flowers with a large

black blotch in the centre of each petal. *P. somniferum* (opium poppy) is taller, to 90cm (3ft), with fleshy, waxy, grey-green leaves, large flowers in pink, mauve, red, purple, and almost black, and decorative seed pods. Double-flowered forms are widely available, with their petals fringed ('Carnation Flowered') or entire ('Paeony Flowered'). Sow in spring; often self-seeds.
☼ ◊ ❋❋❋
P. somniferum ♥ *p.21, p.44*,
P. rhoeas. Shirley Series ♥ *p.31*

Pelargonium
Popular perennials grown as annuals for containers and bedding, with aromatic leaves and long-stalked clusters of flowers in red, pink, purple, orange, and white. Zonal types have rounded leaves marked with a darker band and large heads of single or double flowers. Ivy-leaved types are trailing or climbing with lobed, fairly fleshy leaves and more spidery flowers. Unique types, like 'Voodoo', are shrubby, with pungent leaves and single flowers.
☼ ◊ Hardiness varies

Multibloom Pink ♥ *p.36, p.41*. Also recommended: Diamond Series

Penstemon
Medium to tall, short-lived perennials, often grown as annuals. Usually bushy, with lance-shaped leaves and long, one-sided spikes of tubular to bell-shaped flowers in purple, red, pink, mauve, or white. Many cultivars and seed selections are available. Sow under glass in spring or autumn, or take softwood cuttings in summer.
☼ ◊ ❋❋

Petunia
Bushy, often sticky, short-lived perennials grown as annuals, with oval to elliptical, matt-green leaves and single, frilled, or double, funnel-shaped flowers, some finely scented, in diverse hues. Smaller, bushy types, such as Carpet Series ♥, are excellent for bedding; trailing ones, such as weather-resistant Surfinia Series, are ideal for containers. Sow under glass in early spring.
☼ ◊ ❋
Surfinia Series ♥ *p.43*

PHLOX DRUMMONDII
'PALONA LIGHT SALMON'

Phacelia campanularia
(Californian bluebell)
Compact, bushy annual with oval, deep green leaves and numerous small, bell-shaped, deep blue flowers. Excellent for attracting bees and butterflies. Sow in spring.
☼ ☼ ◊ ✽✽✽

Phlox drummondii
(Annual phlox)
Small, bushy annual with lance-shaped, pale green leaves. Flowers are borne in dense clusters and may be flat-faced and long-throated (as in the Palona Series) or star-shaped, both in a range of pastel or bright colours, often patterned, bicoloured, or zoned. Good for bedding. Sow under glass in spring.
☼ ◊ ✽
'Sternenzauber' p.10

Portulacca grandiflora
(Sun plant)
A low-growing, spreading, fleshy annual with red stems and narrow, pointed, bright green leaves. Bears fairly large, satiny, bowl-shaped, single or double flowers in bright shades of yellow, orange, red, pink, or white. Sow under glass in spring.
☼ ◊ ✽

Psylliostachys suworowii
(Statice)
A medium, erect, fairly slow-growing annual with lobed, lance-shaped leaves and erect, slender, pipe-cleaner spikes of tiny, bright pink flowers, good for drying. Sow in spring under glass, late spring in the open.
☼ ◊ ✽

R

Reseda odorata
(Mignonette)
Medium, pale green, erect to spreading annual, with narrow, oval leaves, and fat spikes of small, greenish white, powerfully scented flowers. Sow seed in spring.
☼ ☼ ◊ ✽✽✽

Ricinus communis
(Castor oil plant)
An imposing evergreen shrub, often grown as an annual for flamboyant bedding schemes

RESEDA ODORATA

RUDBECKIA HIRTA
'RUSTIC DWARFS'

(p.36). The leaves are very large, hand-like, and deep bronze or purplish. Short spikes of small, red flowers precede prickly seed capsules.
☼ ◊ ✽

Rudbeckia hirta
Medium, short-lived perennial (p.30), often grown as an annual, with rough, lance-shaped, mid-green leaves and large, yellow daisies with conical purple centres. Good for cutting. 'Marmalade' has golden flowers with black cones. Sow seed in spring.
☼ ◊ ✽✽✽
'Radiant Gold' p.60

S

Salpiglossis sinuata
Medium, upright, moderately bushy annuals with lance-shaped, sticky, pale green leaves. Flower trumpets are outward-facing, in bright colours, particularly yellow, orange, red, and blue, and are conspicuously veined. Sow under glass in early spring.
☼ ◊ ✽

SALVIA SPLENDENS
'SCARLET KING'

Salvia (Sage)

Square-stemmed annuals or
perennials grown as annuals,
with whorled spikes of showy,
two-lipped flowers. *S. farinacea*
is tall, with lance-shaped
leaves and white, blue, or
violet flower spikes. *S. patens*
♀ is medium, with lax spikes
of large, deep blue flowers.
S. coccinea is tall, with oval,
serrated leaves and red flowers.
S. splendens is low to medium
and bushy with oval, serrated,
fresh-green leaves and dense,
scarlet flowers and bracts.
Cultivars in violet, purple,
pink, white, salmon, or red
(as in 'Scarlet King') all make
excellent bedding. *S. viridis*
(annual clary) is medium
and hardy with pink or pale
flowers tipped by bracts in
blue, purple, pink, or white.
Sow under glass in spring;
sow *S. viridis* in open ground.
☼ ◊ ❋

S. splendens Cleopatra Series
p.36, *S. viridis p.27*

Sanvitalia procumbens
(Creeping zinnia)

A mat-forming, prostrate
annual with oval, pointed,
bright green leaves and many
small, yellow daisies with
black centres. Sow in spring.
☼ ◊ ❋❋❋

Scabiosa (Pincushion flower, Scabious)

Bushy annuals with flat
flowerheads, the outer florets
being the largest. Biennials
and short-lived perennials
are usually grown as annuals.
S. atropurpurea (sweet
scabious) is tall with lance-
shaped leaves and purple,
blue, white, or crimson
flowers. *S. stellata* (starry
scabious) is medium with
lyre-shaped leaves and pale or
pink flowers and decorative,
beige, starry seedheads, good
for drying. Sow in spring.
☼ ◊ ❋❋❋

Scaevola aemula

Low to medium, spreading to
trailing perennial grown as an
annual, with lance-shaped to
oval leaves and clusters of
blue, lilac, violet, or white,
lobelia-like flowers. Excellent
for containers. Sow seed
under glass in spring.
☼ ◊ ❋❋❋
'New Wonder' *p.40*

Schizanthus pinnatus
(Poor man's orchid)

Bushy annuals with feathery
green leaves and large clusters
of showy, orchid-like flowers
in varied hues with contrasting
markings, often with a yellow
or white centre. Excellent in
containers. Sow seed in
spring, or in late summer for
flowering under glass.
☼ ◊ min. 5°C (41°F).

Senecio cineraria

A medium, mound-forming,
evergreen shrub, usually

SENECIO CINERARIA
'SILVER DUST'

grown as an annual, with
handsome, variously lobed,
silver-grey foliage (*p.34*).
Bears clusters of mustard-
yellow flowerheads on long
stalks in the second summer.
☼ ◊ ❋❋

Silene armeria (Campion, Sweet William catchfly)

A small to medium, upright
annual or biennial, with
paired, oval, grey-green leaves
and branched clusters of rose-
pink, star-shaped flowers,
with slightly notched petals,
in summer and early autumn.
Good for butterflies. Sow in
spring or summer.
☼ ◊ ❋❋❋

Silybum marianum (Blessed Mary's thistle)

A tall, coarse biennial that
forms a large, flat leaf-rosette
in the first year. The leaves
are quite broad, deeply lobed,
glossy and spiny, and deep-
green in colour with bold,
white or silver marbling. The
flowers are purple, thistle-
like, and good for drying.
Sow seed in spring.
☼ ◊ ❋❋❋

Rosewarne
Learning Centre

Smyrnium perfoliatum

Medium to tall, erect biennial. The upper leaves and bracts are oval, bright yellow-green, and encircle the stem. Bears small heads of tiny, greenish yellow flowers. Sow in early spring; often self-seeds.

☼ ◊ ✽✽✽

Solanum pseudocapsicum

(Christmas cherry, Jerusalem cherry, Winter cherry) Evergreen, bushy perennial, grown as an annual, with lance-shaped leaves. Small, starry, white flowers precede showy, round, scarlet fruits. Sow under glass in spring.

☼ ◊ ✽✽✽

Solenostemon scutellarioides

(Coleus, Flame nettle) A bushy, evergreen perennial grown as an annual. "Ace-of-spade" leaves are often variegated and marked in vibrant pink, yellow, green, red, or purple, sometimes multicoloured. Remove flower spikes to encourage new shoots. Sow under glass in spring and summer.

☼ ◊ min. 10°C (50°F)
Wizard Series *p.16*

Sutera grandiflora (Purple glory plant)

Small to medium, spreading to trailing perennial with small, toothed, oval leaves and pink, white or purple, frilled, long-throated, flat-faced flowers in summer and autumn. Good container plant. Sow under glass in early spring, or take softwood cuttings in summer.

☼ ◊ min. 5°C (41°F).
'Knysna Hills' *p.42*, **'Sea Mist'** *p.40*

T

Tagetes (Marigold)

Strongly aromatic, stiff, bushy annuals with finely divided foliage and solitary, daisy- or carnation-like flowers. French marigold cultivars, bred from *T. patula*, have single to fully double flowers in yellow, orange, mahogany, or red, or bicoloured or zoned. Popular for bedding and containers. Many varieties are available, from tall to dwarf. African marigold cultivars come from *T. erecta*, a medium to tall plant with large, single to fully double flowers in gold, cream, or orange. Small-flowered Signet marigolds are bred from *T. tenuifolia*. Sow under glass in early spring.

☼ ◊ ✽
'Golden Gem' *p.36*

Tanacetum parthenium

(Feverfew) A medium, bushy biennial or short-lived perennial (*p.18*). The aromatic, deeply lobed, oblong leaves are dark green, but golden-green in 'Aureum'. Bears broad clusters of small, white daisies with gold centres. Sow in spring; often self-seeds.

☼ ◊ ✽✽✽

Thymophylla tenuiloba

(Golden fleece) A medium annual or biennial, with fern-like leaves and small, orange-yellow daisies in late spring and summer. Sow seed in spring.

☼ ◊ ✽✽✽

Tithonia rotundifolia

syn. *T. speciosa* (Mexican sunflower) Tall, upright annual with triangular to oval, often lobed leaves, and 8cm (3in) bright orange or scarlet, zinnia-like

SMYRNIUM PERFOLIATUM

TAGETES 'TANGERINE GEM'

THYMOPHYLLA TENUILOBA

flowerheads. Good for cutting. Sow under glass in spring.

☼ ◊ ✽

Torenia fournieri
(Wishbone flower)
Small, bushy annual (*p.42*) with serrated, elliptical, fairly pale leaves and flared, tubular, two-lipped flowers of pale blue-purple, with purple-black bases. Good container plant. Sow under glass in spring.

☼ ◊ min. 5°C (41°F)
'Blue Moon' *p.16*

Trachelium caeruleum
syn. *Diosphaera caeruleum*
(Blue throatwort) ♀
Tall perennial grown as an annual, with oval, serrated leaves and dense clusters of small, lilac flowers. Good for butterflies and cutting. Sow under glass in early spring.

☼ ◊ ✽

Tropaeolum majus
(Nasturtium)
Dwarf nasturtiums (*see also p.65*) form medium, bushy plants. The flowers are edible. Sow seed in spring, but take stem-tip cuttings of named forms like 'Hermine Grashoff'.

☼ ◊ Hardiness varies
Alaska Series ♀ p.7, **'Hermine Grashoff'** ♀ *p.40*

V

Verbascum olympicum
(Mullein)
Handsome, tall biennial that forms a large, grey-felted rosette in the first year; in the second, many small, bright yellow flowers are borne in branching spires on felted stems. *V. bombyciferum* ♀ is even larger, to 2m (6ft), with

VERBENA 'IMAGINATION'

silver-white foliage. Sow in spring; sometimes self-seeds.

☼ ◊ ✽✽✽

Verbena
Verbena bonariensis is a frost-hardy, tall biennial with sparse, oblong leaves and small, red-purple flowerheads that attract butterflies. Hybrid verbenas, good in containers, are half-hardy, spreading, trailing or bushy perennials, grown as annuals. They have narrow, toothed foliage and dense, flat heads of small flowers in vivid pink, blue, mauve, white, and red, often with yellow or white eyes. Sow under cover in spring.

☼ ◊ Hardiness varies
'Imagination' *p.41*, **'Tapien Pink'** *p.43*

Viola (Pansy)
Low-growing annual or short-lived perennial with toothed, oval leaves and flowers in varied sizes, hues, bicolours, or patterned "faces". Ideal for formal and informal bedding. Sow outdoors in late winter.

☼ ◊ ✽✽✽
'Romeo and Juliet' *p.15*, **'Sorbet Yellow Frost'** *p.39*

X

Xeranthemum annuum
(Immortelle)
A tufted, medium annual with lance-shaped, silver leaves and purple daisies with silver, papery, "everlasting" bracts. Dries well. Sow in spring.

☼ ◊ ✽✽

Z

Zinnia
Zinnia elegans is an upright to bushy annual with rough, oval to lance-shaped leaves and showy flowers mainly in pink, red, purple, yellow, and cream. There are cultivars in all sizes, with single, double or pompon flowerheads; 'Envy' tolerates shade. Good for cutting. *Z. haageana* (Mexican zinnia) is a medium annual with narrow, lance-shaped leaves. Sow under glass in spring, or outdoors in mild areas in late spring.

☼ ◊ ✽
Zinnia elegans 'Dreamland Scarlet' *p.14*, *Zinnia haageana* **'Persian Carpet'** *p.8*

ZINNIA ELEGANS 'ENVY'

INDEX

ACKNOWLEDGMENTS

Picture research Anna Grapes
Picture librarian Neale Chamberlain

Planting plan illustrations Gill Tomblin
Additional illustrations Karen Cochrane

Index Hilary Bird

Dorling Kindersley would like to thank:
All staff at the RHS, in particular Susanne Mitchell, Karen Wilson and Barbara Haynes at Vincent Square; Candida Frith-Macdonald for editorial assistance.

The Royal Horticultural Society
To learn more about the work of the Society, visit the RHS on the Internet at **www.rhs.org.uk**.

Information includes news of events around the country, a horticultural database, international plant registers, results of plant trials and membership details.

Photography
The publisher would like to thank the following for their kind permission to reproduce their photographs (key: t=top, b=bottom, r=right, c=centre):

John Glover: back cover tl and b, 6, 8tl, 9t, 10br, 11t, 11b, 12b, 13t, 13b, 16b, 17tr, 18, 19b, 21t, 23tl, 25b, 25tl, 35, 38, 39; **Christopher Grey-Wilson:** 5br, 15tl, 25tr, 26bl, 27t; **Photos Horticultural:** front cover r, back cover tr, 4bl, 9b, 15bl, 23tr, 28, 29, 34; **Daan Smit:** 2, 10bl, 14br, 14bc, 15r, 19t, 27b.